STUDIES OF FAMOUS BIBLE WOMEN

Studies of Famous Bible Women

By
HENRY T. SELL, D.D.

*Author of The Sell Series of Bible Study Books
for Adult and Teacher Training Bible
Classes, Schools, Colleges
and Private Study.*

1089

NEW YORK   CHICAGO

Fleming H. Revell Company

LONDON   AND   EDINBURGH

Printed in the United States of America

New York: 158 Fifth Avenue
Chicago: 17 North Wabash Ave.
London: 21 Paternoster Square
Edinburgh: 75 Princes Street

FOREWORD

THIS is a woman's age. She is coming into her rights and taking the place which belongs to her.

This place has not been won, solely, by education, agitation, demand or entreaty but, in the main, by the wide dissemination of Scriptural ideals and standards for women.

It is a well known fact that it is only, in the lands where these ideals have a free circulation, that the advanced position of woman has been accorded to her.

The best Bible women are well worth the most careful study as they are the acknowledged trailblazers for the larger freedom of thought and action. In this book we consider certain aspects of their lives and careers which bring out, in a clear light, their important contributions to the present high status, destined to go higher, of womankind.

The worst Bible women—human nature does not change—serve to mark the dangerous shoals, quicksands and rocks of life, where their lives were wrecked, and which still exist as death traps.

The purpose is to take the narratives, in their forms, as we find them, and to get directly at the truths, the meanings and the teachings which the authors and compilers attempted to express. Very definite present-day applications are made.

These women succeeded in getting their messages of uplift, encouragement and warning across to their own generation, and to ours, in a most remarkable way. They stand out of their race and times as no other women stand out.

This book is a short course of Bible study showing the very important part women have had in its history.

Twenty-one of the most typical women are selected for these *Studies of Famous Bible Women,* such as Eve, Rebekah, Deborah, Delilah, Jezebel, Queen of Sheba, Mother of Jesus, Mary and Martha, the wife of Peter, Lydia and others.

For original class work it is suggested that studies be made of the lives of Sarah, Rachel, Rizpah, Naaman's Little Captive Maid, Rhoda, Priscilla and others not considered in this book.

This is the companion volume to the author's *Studies of Great Bible Characters* (Men), and the twelfth in his series of Bible study books.

It is for use in Adult Bible and Teacher Training Classes, Schools, Colleges, private study, etc.

H. T. S.

New York, N. Y.

Contents

I. EVE 9
The New Woman.

II. REBEKAH 17
Romance and Common Sense.

III. JOCHEBED AND MIRIAM . . . 24
Resolute, Resourceful Women.

IV. DEBORAH 31
An Able Leader of Men.

V. DELILAH 38
A Temptress.

VI. RUTH 45
A Dependable Woman.

VII. HANNAH 53
Mother of a Great Prophet.

VIII. QUEEN OF SHEBA 60
The Seeker After Wisdom.

IX. WIDOW OF ZAREPHATH . . . 67
Faith Under Difficulties.

X. JEZEBEL 74
The Ruthless Queen.

XI. ESTHER 81
Self-sacrifice For a Cause.

XII. WOMAN OF SOLOMON'S SONG . . 90
The Single Standard.

8   Contents

XIII. MOTHER OF JESUS 97
Best and Best Known.

XIV. WIFE OF PETER 106
A Hidden Woman.

XV. WOMAN OF SAMARIA . . . 113
A Keen Questioner.

XVI. MARTHA AND MARY 120
A Task and a Vision.

XVII. MARY MAGDALENE 127
A Woman of Large Service.

XVIII. MOTHER OF JAMES AND JOHN . . 134
An Ambitious Woman.

XIX. DORCAS 141
A Philanthropic Woman.

XX. MARY, MOTHER OF MARK . . 148
An Influential Church Worker.

XXI. LYDIA 154
A Business Woman.

I

EVE

THE NEW WOMAN

The Story of Eve is the oldest one of womankind in the Bible.

It fairly bristles with historical, scientific and theological difficulties. It is embedded in the chapters which have been battle-grounds for centuries. Taken as it reads, at face value, and laying aside the controversies, we find it replete, as a story, with the most intense human and religious interests.

It is strikingly dramatic in its representation of the perplexing crises, or stages of development, through which Eve is declared to have passed.

The Position of the New Woman is made plain. The same claim is made for the high origin of woman as that of man—Genesis 1 : 27. She is represented, all through the narrative, as thinking and acting independently—Chapters 2-4.

Woman is Shown as man's equal, companion and helpmeet—Genesis 2 : 18, 23.

There is not a trace, here, of the Oriental idea of the inferiority, the degradation and slave notion—the shame and disgrace of the world—which were forced upon her later on.

The Sacredness of the Law of "The Pair Marriage" is proclaimed at the outset. It is the great goal sought to-day. If universally adopted it would make over society, reform governments and do away with untold evils and miseries. Adam said of his wife—" This is now bone of my bones and flesh of my flesh. . . . Therefore shall a man leave his father and mother, and shall cleave unto his wife and they shall be one flesh "—Genesis 2: 23, 24.

Jesus Christ quotes, commends and sanctions this, " The Law " that works for the greatest happiness—Matthew 19: 4-6.

This ideal of marriage was proclaimed long before Israel had a name and a place in the world. This people departed from it in " Patriarchal Polygamy " and suffered the consequences.

The Most Ardent Advocate of Woman's Freedom and Rightful Place, in the world, can not go beyond what is here set forth. The trouble has been, in studying these early chapters of Genesis, that the attention has been focussed upon the mysteries and difficulties rather than upon the great truths which are so plainly taught.

Stages of Development.—The story of Eve is very condensed. Every word is made to count at its full value and needs to be studied carefully to get its meaning not only in itself but also in connection with its fellows. The word pictures are masterpieces ; each one complete, yet representing but one of a series. We must look at them all, in turn, to get the full importance of the things they teach. They show the " Stages of Development " through which " The New Woman " passed.

The Age of Innocence and spontaneity. We first see Eve in a beautiful garden, " Eastward in Eden." What a wonderful picture it is ! Our imagination glorifies the few details given us. We behold smiling skies ; we are delighted with the sight of beautiful flowers and we inhale their perfume. There are trees, good for food, and good to look at. Singing birds, charming us with their sweet songs, are everywhere. Every prospect pleases. Yet this fascinating place is not one of idleness for Adam and Eve are to dress it and to keep it—Genesis 2: 8-15.

This period in the life of Eve, although she is represented as a grown woman, has been compared to that of a young girl, who in her simplicity and innocence, is spontaneous and free in all her thoughts and actions. She has not yet awakened to what is in her and before her. She is, as yet untried, for her life is a securely sheltered one. She has no inkling of her powers and possibilities; they are there but undeveloped.

There are "Gardens of Eden" in many modern households and the Eves are there. This is not an affair of yesterday but also of to-day.

The Time of Testing and temptation—Genesis 3: 1-6. The picture is not a pleasant one. Dark clouds are gathering. There is a chill in the air. The birds have ceased to sing. This to us; to Eve, listening to a persuasive voice, telling her of very much better things outside and beyond the confines of the garden, there are no dark clouds and no chill in the air.

She is being told that this garden, which she has thought so much of, is a prison. To really enjoy things she must break out of it and realize the full possibilities of her life. She is told that her God wants to keep her back from the enjoyment of her full possibilities. Why be kept back? Why wait? Eat of the tree of knowledge of good and evil and be a God yourself. Take your life in your own hands and enjoy every appetite to the full.

She has been told, on the other hand, that she must not force matters of growth—Genesis 2: 17; 3: 1-6.

But the persuasive voice of the serpent in this and every Eden, tells her that she, in substance, is old-fashioned, if we may so call it, and nothing whatever will happen if she breaks over a law of her nature and of her God—Genesis 3: 4, 5.

We know what happened to Eve, when she yielded to the temptation to " An upward fall."

Possibilities can be developed only in legitimate ways. Growth cannot be forced. You cannot get a full blown rose by picking open a bud or a great oak by dissecting an acorn.

This Story Is Modern in every respect.—Eve Bascom of Cherry Valley grew up to womanhood before her parents hardly realized it. They were very good to Eve. She was an only child. Everything was done for her. But she became very much dissatisfied. She felt that she was being held back. The serpent had come into her garden of Eden with the same old, old story. One night, after her parents had gone to bed, she stole out of the house, with her satchel, and took the train for the big city. The rest of the story? It is written on the police blotter of one more of " The Unfortunates."

Eve Jackson Jones, wife of a prominent merchant, lived a sheltered life. She had everything heart could wish. A very slick handsome young man saw her. He desired her. He played the part that was played in the old garden long ago. It worked not for a larger life but for a broken-up home and the wreck of the young wife. It all came out in the divorce court.

The Threefold Trial of a Soul.—This story of

Eve's temptation has been compared to that of Christ —Matthew 4:1-11. Both have the same Tempter, while not in the same order.

First—Addressed to The Bodily Appetites.—Eve saw that " The tree was good for food "—Genesis 3:6. Compare, Matthew 4:3, " And when the tempter came to him (Jesus Christ) he said, If thou be the Son of God, command that these stones be made bread." That was when Christ was an hungered. Here is the cry of " The evil-minded man " to-day. He says, " Gratify every bodily appetite." He means it. He advocates this doctrine. He practises it. It is of no consequence to him how many wrecks he makes of other people. He only thinks of himself. He is a hostile submarine on the high seas of life, seeking only to destroy. Science to-day has united with the Bible in teaching the importance of keeping under the bodily appetites; for, given unrestrained rein, they cause untold damage.

Second—Addressed to The Sense of Beauty.—Eve saw that " The tree . . . was pleasant to the eyes "—Genesis 3:6 Compare, Matthew 4:8-10. " Again the devil taketh him (Jesus Christ) up into an exceeding high mountain, and sheweth him all the kingdoms of the world, and the glory of them. And said unto him, All these things will I give thee if thou wilt fall down and worship me." See Christ's answer —Matthew 4:10.

Often the worst evils seek to lure by sheer beauty. No one, even the most depraved, is attracted by bare and ugly sins, seen in all their hideousness. Every swindler plies his trade under the guise of being a beautiful and bountiful benefactor.

It is the delight of the eyes, beyond what one can afford in extravagance of living, seeing and going, that leads to destruction. This is a present-day temptation. Better clothes than one can afford, pearls, diamonds, entertainments; all have a drawing power which is like a powerful magnet to the iron in every one of us.

We are taken up on a mountain and shown the glory, not the poverty, not the sin, not the misery of the world, but its glittering beauty. No man can say but what he is attracted away from his humdrum tasks by this glory. This is not the beauty of service or sacrifice which Christ taught and that which can alone benefit and lift up our fellow-men, with ourselves, to a higher level.

Third—Addressed to The Desire for Wisdom.— Eve saw " A tree to be desired to make one wise "— Genesis 3: 6. Compare, Matthew 4: 5-7, where Jesus is placed upon a pinnacle of the temple and bidden to cast Himself down in the trust that angels will bear Him up.

A spiritual and mental temptation. To be wise above God. To know what is best for us above the Divine Wisdom. It is to pray not God's will but my will be done, never mind God, to say nothing of our fellow-men.

To seek wisdom is a natural desire. What better can we do than to multiply our schools and colleges to this end of knowing more?

The lure of every temptation is that it proceeds along a line that is legitimate and right, up to a certain point. This is the attractive bait that conceals the hook which will presently be jerked and we will

be caught. The bait is, in short, that wisdom by
which we can be placed on high and overrule and
override others.

Eve placed her wisdom, as to the eating of the fruit
of the tree of knowledge of good and evil, above that
of God.

The Crisis.—The independence of Eve, and her
freedom of choice, is shown in that she, according to
the narrative, did not talk over the matter with her
husband. She knew just what she ought to do and
repeated it to the Tempter—Genesis 3:2, 3. This is
the pitiful part of this whole matter of going into sin.
Eve knew what was right but made the deliberate
choice of evil.

Then the matter followed the same course that it
follows to-day.

The Aftermath.—After the yielding to temptation, nothing seemed to happen. Eve might have said
—" See I have crossed the line between good and evil
and nothing has come of it." But wait! It did not
take long for things to begin to happen, and when
they did—Genesis 3:8-24—Adam and Eve found
themselves outside the gates of Paradise and hard put
to it to make a living where the land produced thorns
and thistles—Genesis 3:18.

This story repeats itself every day. It reads something like this, in the morning's newspaper: Mr. and
Mrs. Adam and Eve Snedeker Jackson, through il-
legitimate practices, described last week, have been
compelled to give up their beautiful villa in Paradise
Park and have gone to live on the South side of the
city, across the street from the municipal dumping
ground.

The Promise and Possibility of Recuperation.—Notice three actions ascribed to God. They are important.

First—He Gave Them a Full Hearing.—He let them tell their side of their story. They were not condemned unheard—Genesis 3: 7-13.

Second—He Condemned the Tempter and Gave a Promise and a Possibility of Recuperation before He pronounced the punishment for the sin—Genesis 3: 14, 15. Here is no hard, stern God but one who seeks the return of wrong-doers, through repentance.

Third—Only After a Full Hearing, Condemnation of the Tempter and a Promise of Recuperation, He Pronounces the Dooms—Genesis 3: 16-24—which are by no means easy to bear.

Did Eve Return, with Her Husband, to the Favour of God?—A careful reading of the after narrative, as it is set down, makes us believe that she did.

Note: In the first two chapters of his book (*Bible Study by Periods*), "Creation" and "The Garden of Eden," the author has taken up some of the more difficult problems of the first chapters of Genesis; the treatments of which are outside his purpose in this book.

Questions.—What can be said about the story of Eve? What about the position of "The New Woman"; her equality with man; her independence; the "Pair-Marriage"? Describe the stages of development; the "Age of Innocence"; the "Time of Testing." Give an account of "The Threefold Trial of a Soul"; addressed to the "Bodily Appetites"; the "Sense of Beauty"; the "Desire for Wisdom." What can be said of the "Crisis"; the "Aftermath"; the "Promise and Possibility of Recuperation"? Did Eve return to the favour of God?

II

REBEKAH

ROMANCE AND COMMON SENSE

Romance plays a leading part in a number of Bible Narratives. The story of Rebekah—Genesis 24—is one of them. It opens with an unexpected proposal of marriage. The desires of an old man for his son and of an eligible young man, for happiness, are fulfilled. The dreams of a young woman, "Very fair to look upon," are realized.

Here romance dons her most festive garments and assumes her most cheerful countenance. Everything combines to make a love story of singular power and sweetness. If we only half look for it we will see how often this sort of a thing comes to the surface. Our Lord made His first public appearance at a wedding. There is a craving, in all hearts, for this light of joy out of the ordinary routine of humdrum every-day realities.

Common Sense.—Taken, on the other hand, this narrative moves along, what may be called, the most calculated estimates of causes and effects. Everything is considered before Abraham sends out his servant, "That ruled over all he had" to seek a wife for his son, Isaac. The chances of success and defeat, of the project, are carefully canvassed. Minute instructions are given of where to go and what to do. Common Sense is applied to a very difficult problem. Everything possible to foresee is foreseen and provided for.

Is There Any Antagonism Between Romance and Common Sense? There ought not to be. Each is necessary to the other, as it is shown in this narrative.

Romance, without common sense, no matter how high and exalted it may be, soon comes crashing to the ground, a crushed and broken thing.

That is an every-day modern event.

Common sense can not rise from the earth without the wings of romance.

The Plan.—There are things Abraham wished to see accomplished. There were things he wanted to avoid. He desired his son Isaac to be happily married: as he was afterwards to Rebekah. He did not want him to take a wife of the alien people around him. He had seen too much misery result from such marriages.

It was the custom of the times, as it is now in Eastern countries, for parents to choose marriage mates for their children. It is quite evident that Abraham talked over the matter with Isaac for he knew all about the project of the camel caravan, under the guidance of Eliezer, to look him up a wife.

The Problem of Suitability in Marriage, which Abraham and Isaac had before them, is an exceedingly modern one.

Here is what a great authority, on marriage to-day, has to say in a recent magazine review of this question—" There ought to be selection in marriage by equality of breeding, and of culture, in the same mores, so as to assure sympathy in ideas, standards, aims and modes of life of the spouses of those who have to spend their lives together. There should also be selection by health and character for the sake of the children that they may be well brought up."

Abraham went farther than this authority. He wanted the same standard in morals and religion without which the others are apt to fail. In this he showed himself, in a more advanced position, than the above quoted magazine writer. He is a man who carefully considered one of the greatest problems of the ages, in all its bearings.

The Executive Eliezer.—He was a wise old man. He took the caravan which was large and imposing, after getting the most careful instructions as to how to proceed, and headed towards the old home town where Abraham's kin lived in the city of Nahor in Mesopotamia. Arrived; notice the fact that he did not go at once to a relative's house. He prayed over the matter and asked that the Lord direct him. It would be an excellent thing if there were more of this. He then waited. He wanted to see the young marriageable women off their guard. He proposed to see what he had to choose from, before making himself known. There could not be more care taken in selection than this.

Rebekah Appears, coming to draw water, at the common well. She was "Very fair to look upon." She was the daughter of "Bethuel, the son of Milcah, the wife of Nahor, Abraham's brother." Rebekah seemed to fulfill all the conditions of "Suitability," in what he had prayed for.

1   She was a beautiful young woman.

2   She had a kind disposition. She at once gave him to drink, as he asked her, from the water which she drew from the well.

3   She not only did this but she offered to draw water from the well for ten camels. Now to do this was no slight task.

She did more than was asked of her with no ulterior motive, for as yet she did not know Eliezer or his mission. It is not often that a person is found who will go out of their way to do so big a favour.

She showed that she had great physical strength in drawing water for so many thirsty camels to drink.

She was hospitality itself, for on being asked to lodge Eliezer and his caravan, she at once responded with a most cordial invitation to her father's house.

She passed the final test when, on being questioned, she showed who she was and to what family she belonged.

Negotiations Proceeded with Great Swiftness. Eliezer, the shrewd, does not hesitate a moment to invest Rebekah—Genesis 24:22—with the betrothal earring and bracelets. He goes at once to her home and in the most matter of fact, common-sense way, tells all about his mission and his master, Abraham and his son, Isaac. He enlarges upon Isaac's prospects as the sole heir of Abraham. He tells, doubtless, of his excellent qualities as a man and of his physical beauty. Trust Eliezer not to leave anything unsaid of the desirability of this union, and of his master's son, that ought to be said. He formally asks for Rebekah's hand, in marriage, for Isaac. Then he wants to be off at once—the very next day.

Rebekah's Acceptance. The family want her to remain at least ten days. But Eliezer is exceedingly urgent for a departure the next morning. Rebekah consents to the early date for leaving. Here is " Romance " with a big " R ". Consider how Rebekah's heart must have been stirred! How all the dreams she had dreamed of this event of which every normal young woman does think more or less, had now come true. Going out one afternoon to draw water, as she had done on so many afternoons, and the very next day, at the same hour, on her way to get married to a very desirable young man. Yet, in it all, there had come the most common sense, most suitable arrangements, for present and future welfare.

The Meeting of Rebekah and Isaac.—In due time the caravan reached the homeland. Isaac, as anxious to see his future wife, as she is to see him, is on the lookout. No details are given of that meeting but it must have seemed to them almost as if they had known each other a long, long time.

A Happy Home.—It must have been a happy home for Rebekah perfectly satisfied Isaac. He is the only one of the patriarchs, who according to the degenerate custom of the times and country, did not take another wife. A home is not in the largeness of the house, the decorations, the number of servants but in the love which husband and wife bear for each other.

A Cloud Arises on the Horizon of this happy home with the coming of " The World Famous Twins," Esau and Jacob. If a man had been writing a novel he would have closed this charming love story with the meeting of Isaac and Rebekah and their marriage. But this is a Bible writer and he is writing of life which sometimes has its bitter trials beyond the young and middle aged periods. The story is told in Genesis 25:20; 33:20, etc. Read the first few chapters and the cloud seems to grow bigger and bigger, yet if you read on far enough you see how the cloud clears away in the blessings that come to Jacob and to his sons and the further history of Israel.

Why Did This Cloud Arise?   Esau and Jacob were much thought of when they were little. As they grew up to manhood they developed entirely different dispositions. " Esau was a cunning hunter, a man of the field: Jacob was a plain man dwelling in tents."

Esau was the favourite of Isaac. Jacob was the one beloved by his mother. Each parent tried to advance the child beloved. Rebekah, having the quickest brain, so managed affairs that Jacob got the parental blessing which would have naturally gone to Esau.

Rebekah clouded the happiness of the home because out of the very intenseness of her love for Jacob she tried to play Providence for him. She put herself in the place of God. She tried to bend things that did not naturally bend the way she wanted them to. She deceived Isaac into thinking that he was blessing Esau when he was blessing Jacob. To be sure Jacob was much better fitted to carry out the conditions of the birthright but that did not excuse Rebekah.

But it is here that many another mother has erred. She has tried, as Rebekah did, to play God for one child above another and to show partiality where no partiality should exist. It may be that this is the reason why this cloud on the home of Isaac and Rebekah is shown to exist.

Rebekah's Punishment.   When Esau found that he had lost the blessing of the first born, he was very angry. Isaac was not at all pleased to find that he had been duped. Things were not very pleasant in that formerly happy home. Rebekah, with her sensitive, strong disposition, could find little to comfort her. Finally things became so unpleasant that Jacob was compelled to leave his father's house and he did not return for fourteen years. Without the comfort of Jacob's presence, of whom she thought so much, there was not very much to cheer the heart of his mother. She erred through the very intensity of her love to have things come out the way she thought they ought to come out. Without her playing Providence, Jacob might still have come to the larger things.

The Character of Rebekah.—Here is no veiled shrinking Oriental woman, but one in whom the strong, rugged traits predominate. She is a vigorous personality. She is clever, active and energetic. She is quick to make decisions and she does not hesitate in carrying them out. She seeks to dominate events rather than have them dominate her. She is strong and masterful from the time she appears in the Scriptural narrative until she goes out.

Questions.—What can be said about romance playing a leading part in the Bible? What can be said about common sense? Are they antagonistic? What can be said about the plan of Abraham? What about suitability in marriage? Who was Eliezer, and what did he do? Describe Rebekah's appearance, and her excellencies. What can be said about the swiftness of the negotiations for her marriage and Rebekah's acceptance. Describe the meeting of Isaac and Rebekah; the happy home; the cloud on the horizon and how it came. What of Rebekah's punishment? Describe Rebekah's character.

III

JOCHEBED AND MIRIAM

RESOLUTE, RESOURCEFUL WOMEN

The Mother and Sister of Moses, Jochebed and Miriam, were resolute and resourceful.

These two qualities are necessary to the successful carrying out of any plan that may be conceived.

A woman may be resolute but utterly lacking in resources, of heart and mind, to bring to a right conclusion that which may seem to her the needed thing to be done.

Again there may be abundant resources but no resolution to marshal them into action which compels attention and breaks down opposition.

The Life of a Nation is at Stake. (Exodus 1st ch.).—The Israelitish nation, since the death of Joseph, who ruled over Egypt, has been degraded to slavery. The people have been compelled to do the hard and menial work for a mighty empire.

In spite of the oppressive tasks forced upon them, their numbers are multiplying so rapidly as to cause serious alarm lest they rise in rebellion, and ally themselves with the enemies of their taskmasters. This alarm causes the Egyptians to devise new methods to make their " lives bitter with hard bondage, in morter and in brick and in all manner of service in the field: all their service, wherein they made them serve, was with rigour."

Unable to check the increase of the Israelites, by hard bondage, the king of Egypt determines on the most drastic measures. He sends out a decree that all the new born male babies shall be destroyed. This is striking at the life of the nation. It is quite evident from the narrative, that " Searchers " are appointed to go through every home and see that the decree is enforced.

A Woman and a Girl, to the Rescue!—What can they do? Blot out now the intervening story between the rescue of the infant Moses, from death, and his leading of the Israelites out of bondage and the whole matter savours of a mighty miracle.

What can a woman and a girl do in such a crisis? We know what they actually did. They saved the infant Moses, by their resoluteness and resourcefulness, from being killed, according to the decree of the Egyptian king, and put him under the care of his daughter. Here is no miracle, or thought of a miracle, but the acme of resourcefulness in a difficult situation. *Thus early do we see the important part given to and carried out by women of the Bible.* The record of this great transaction is not yet written out in full.

The Special Part of Jochebed and her eight-year-old daughter, Miriam, is told in the second chapter of Exodus. The narrative is very brief. Yet by it, the mother of Moses, in the ability to plan and carry out her plan, stands out as one of the great women, not only of the Bible, but of the world. She stamped her ability upon her three remarkable children—Moses, the foremost figure of " The Law "; Aaron, the leading light in " Religion "; Miriam, a great poetess, prophetess and welfare worker. Amram was the father—Numbers 26:59.

When Moses Was Born, Jochebed managed to hide him from "The Egyptian Searchers" for three months. When she found she could hide him no longer, she set her wits to work. There could have been no better plan than that which she finally worked out. She must have smiled at the thought of getting the king of Egypt's daughter to rescue her little son and have him brought up in Pharaoh's court.

Note the careful detail with which the plan is worked out and the shrewdness of the observations beforehand. She must observe the Egyptian princess, that she liked children and the time when she came to bathe. Some one must be on hand when Moses is found to suggest the mother as a nurse for the child. Meantime an ark of bulrushes must be made and the infant placed in it at just the right point in the river where the princess would be sure to see it. Miriam is set to watch to see that no harm comes to the babe and things go as planned.

What could be more natural than that a little girl, eight years old, should come near when the princess finds the child? Again, what could be more natural, doubtless prompted by her mother, than that Miriam should suggest a nurse for the child and that nurse, without mentioning the fact, should be her mother.

Note that Jochebed was not content to have the life of her child saved, she wanted him saved to his nationality, as an Israelite, and to his religion. Without she had become his nurse, Moses would have been brought up, from infancy, as an Egyptian and been lost to his people. If this is not foreseeing things and forelooking after things, we do not know what is.

What need we say more of Jochebed? Her prominent place in the Bible gallery is secure.

The After Career of Miriam.—This part is recorded many years later, when the Children of Israel, following the " Plagues " and the demands of Moses, have been rescued from bondage and passing through " The Red Sea," have reached the other side.

She Had a Very Prominent Part in the Leadership of the Nation. This is quite evident from the scattered notices in the accounts.

She Remained Unmarried. This is quite remarkable when so much attention is given, in these early narratives to marrying and the ill and the good that comes from it. When we look back to the lives of the Patriarchs' wives, we see much space in the records given to them. In Sarah, Abraham's wife, emphasis is laid on this question; in Rebekah, Isaac's wife, there is a long account of the proposal of marriage; in Rachel the keynote is struck in the fourteen years' courtship that preceded her alliance with Jacob.

In the account of Miriam's life, the subject of marriage is so far in the background that it is not even mentioned.

She is a Prophetess—Exodus 15 : 20. " One who delivers the Divine message and interprets the Divine will."

She is a Poetess. Poetry is an art with her not for art's sake, but for the sake of God and humanity. " She is the first of the sweet singers of Israel. She sings for God. She uses her gift for the elevation of human souls into the heavenly life. She becomes in this, the forerunner of all the Hebrew poets."

It has been said that the " Difference between the Jew and the Greek is not in their estimate of artistic beauty, but in the field where they plant that beauty. To the Greek it is an end in itself; to the Jew it is a minister to God. . . . Nothing is painted to show its colour, nothing is sung to reveal its harmony, nothing is written to display its genius; all is for the glory of God."

The great song, found in Exodus 15th ch., is ascribed to Miriam. " It is divided into two parts. Up to the end of the twelfth verse it is historical. The remainder expresses the high hopes inspired by the recent great experiences, in the deliverance from Egypt. Nothing now seems impossible; the fiercest tribes of the desert and of Palestine may be despised. . . . The poem is steeped in gratitude. In the great deliverance, man has borne no part. It is Jehovah who has triumphed gloriously."

She is a Welfare Worker. She is devoted, all the time and always, to what will be for the best interests of her people.

She is an Ardent Patriot—Numbers 12: 1-16. Her sin and rebellion against her brother, Moses, is caused by an excess of zeal for what she considers the welfare of her people. Moses has married an Ethiopian woman and Miriam fears what has come to pass, in many cases, that this woman of an alien nation and different religion, will win her brother away from his religion and his God. Then, too, in the case of her own brother, she may not have had as high an opinion of him as others had. Relatives, especially close relatives, are not apt to esteem too highly the exalted positions of their kin. Miriam was mistaken in the estimate of her brother's loyalty to his country and his God. For that sin she suffered and was punished.

Miriam is the Forerunner of the modern women, who remaining unmarried, devote their time, attention, talents and energies to some profession or pursuit for the general welfare. The more carefully we look over her career, the more clearly it is seen how all her thoughts are given to the uplift of her people.

An Advocate of Woman's Rights.—This has been charged in her favour and against it. Anyway, as the record stands, in the twelfth chapter of Numbers, when she thought that Moses was going to fail, on account of his Ethiopian wife, she felt herself perfectly competent to take his place and boldly told him so. She was deeply concerned, for the national welfare.

Women in offering themselves for elective positions in our country to-day, say that they feel themselves able to take on and perform the duties that will devolve upon them, and prove it by their election to the offices they seek. But, in the case of Miriam, she erred in her estimate of her brother. In our next study, of Deborah, this matter is again to the front. Miriam was certainly in the advance guard of modern women.

Character.—We have in Miriam, a clever woman, with a brilliant mind. She is energetic, resolute, and resourceful. In many respects she was in advance of her times. She is devoted, whole-heartedly to her God and her people.

Questions.—What can be said about the mother and sister of Moses? How was the life of the nation at stake? How did a woman and a girl come to the rescue? What was the special part of Jochebed? What can be said of the after career of Miriam? What about her prominent place; her unmarried state? What can be said about her, as a prophetess, as a poetess, as a welfare worker, an ardent patriot? Of what is Miriam the forerunner? Was she an advocate of woman's rights? What can be said of her character?

IV

DEBORAH

AN ABLE LEADER OF MEN

The First Woman Leader of Men, in the Bible, is Deborah—Judges 4th-5th chs. She became the deliverer of her nation after it had been oppressed and overrun by its enemies for twenty years. She felt the Divine call to action when no man would stand up to the task. Men were afraid to lift their hands or even make a protest against the iniquities of those who lorded it over them.

She was a woman with all the characteristics of a strong man. She called herself " A Mother in Israel "—Judges 5 : 7. She has been called " A Woman with Public Spirit." After she had stirred her people to a realization of their evil condition, she endeavoured to get Barak, a trained man of war, to lead an army against the enemy, but he felt the task so hopeless that he declared he would not do it, unless Deborah went with him. There was nothing for Deborah to do except to take command of the situation. She did this with such effectiveness that the land had rest for " Forty Years."

That Deborah took and occupied the position she did is all the more remarkable from the fact that her age was one in which men, and men alone, were considered competent to head large enterprises.

The Deeds of Deborah are written in two of the twenty-one chapters of the Book of Judges. Of the fifteen leaders, whose exploits are set down, she is the only woman. She is the third in order. This Book of Judges is the history of the transition time, of several hundreds of years, from the death of Joshua—Judges 2:8—to the rise of the great prophet Samuel. The key-note of the " Book " is found in 2:16-19.

The problems to be met were principally three. The way Deborah met them brings out, into a strong light, her great personality, ability and faith.

Problem One—Political. In the desert wandering there had been a strong central authority under Moses. In conquering the Promised Land, Joshua had maintained strict military discipline. With these mighty men dead, the tribes seem to have fallen apart. There was no central government, no king and no fixed capitol. The supremacy passed from one tribe to another as occasion or necessity arose. Again the change in the life of the people from " The Nomadic " in the desert to " The Agricultural and Town Life" was no easy one. The former inhabitants of the land, who had been conquered and thrust aside, were ready to take every advantage to harass and get the Israelites out. There was extreme bitterness of feeling. It is a marvel that they were able to maintain themselves.

Problem Two—Social. The Canaanites remaining, naturally became the teachers in the management of the land and the manner of living. The Israelites adopted many of their evil customs. There were intermarriages. All sorts of trouble arose.

Problem Three—Religious. The Canaanitish religion, easy and seductive, ministered to the evil propensities in man. It was a constant stumbling-block as the religion of Jehovah required purity in life and character. Consider these problems and note how great the task was of this " Leader of Men."

The Fear of the Enemy was over all. The Israelites did not dare to even walk along the highways lest they be robbed and maltreated—Judges 5 : 6. They sought the by-ways in order that they might go in comparative safety. The enemy was malignant in his persecutions. He placed archers not far from the wells and commanded them to shoot at those who came to draw water—Judges 5 : 11. He took away the shields and the spears of the Israelites that they might not be able to defend themselves—Judges 5 : 8. In order that any rebellion on the part of the Israelites could be put down quickly, the captain of the enemy host was provided with nine hundred chariots of iron—Judges 4 : 3. Sisera, the name of the captain, caused men's faces to blanch with fear. He was ruthless and cruel to the last degree. No wonder that the men who knew Sisera dreaded him and refused to go against him.

Deborah, Under the Palm Tree, Tries to Hearten the People.—Her supremacy seems to have arisen in the most natural way, outside her call to leadership by her God. " And Deborah, a prophetess, the wife of Lapidoth, she judged Israel at that time. And she dwelt under the palm tree of Deborah between Ramah and Beth-el in Mount Ephraim: and the children of Israel came up to her for judgment"— Judges 4 : 4, 5.

She was a woman of strong human sympathies. She was greatly stirred by what she heard and saw of the oppressive measures of the enemy of her people. Her career, doubtless, began in her ability to give good, practical advice to those who came to her under her palm tree, at the close of her day's work.

Her heart was stirred by the indignities of the enemy which were told to her.

There were probably three stages through which she passed—

" *The Sympathetic.*" She called herself " A Mother in Israel "—Judges 5:7. She took other peoples' troubles on herself and tried to find a way out for them. She comforted and heartened them. She sent them back home with new courage. There are such women in every community. They are great blessings.

" *The Solemn.*" She warned those who came to be careful not to give occasion to the oppressors so that they might afflict them.

" *The Drastic.*" There came a time when Deborah saw that the enemies of her people were bent on nothing less than extermination. Her heart was hot with indignation. The people of Israel were crying unto God for deliverance—Judges 4:3. Just then her Divine call came which she has described in her song—Judges 5:12. God is moving her to action. There is no doubt that something must be done, and she decides on strong measures.

Strong Arm Methods are Decided Upon by Deborah. The time for compromise has passed. How can there be any compromise when one people deliberately sets out to destroy another?

" This Leader of Men " is not at all anxious to put herself where men have always had the place. She will not now if she can avoid it. She has had no

experience in commanding an army. Note her good
sense! She sends for Barak, a man skilled in the
practice of arms, and one who knows how to put
soldiers in battle array—Judges 4:6.

Just here an unexpected difficulty arises. Barak
has all the military skill, all the experience, and all the
knowledge, but he is lacking in courage. He refuses
to go unless Deborah goes with him. Deborah must
have smiled, even in the midst of her perplexities, at
this man, skilled in the game of warfare, refusing to
go unless she went with him.

Deborah does not hesitate one moment in saying
she will go with him. But she grimly says that there
shall come no honour to him out of the victory that
will surely be his. A woman shall have the honour.

The Joining of the Battle.—Read over what has
gone before, of the sad plight of the Israelites, kept
under the heel of their oppressors for twenty years,
compelled to go in the by-ways, disarmed, scorned and
maltreated and then ask—" How will the battle
turn?" There seems to be, humanly speaking, but
one answer and that is—" A Crushing Defeat."

The narrative seems to imply in the fourth chapter
—4:14—that Barak faltered in the presence of the
foe and that Deborah went to the rescue. Certainly
there is no shadow of doubt cast on Deborah as a
" Leader of Men " under the most difficult conditions.

The Victory (Judges 4:15-24).—What a triumph it was! " And the Lord discomfited Sisera, and
all his chariots and all his host." What rejoicing there
must have been! Now people could go along the highways without danger. The young women could draw
water at the wells without being shot at. A peace of

forty years follows, so sweeping was the victory. In reading the Book of Judges, we sometimes forget how condensed the narrative is. Here are only two short chapters to tell this wonderful story of fortitude and faith and of what a woman did when men lost courage and hope.

The Song of Triumph (Judges, 5th ch.).—Here Deborah shows us another side and that of a poetess of the highest order. She is carried away, and we are with her, to the heights of patriotic fervour which are remarkable. And yet this song is so written that we see in it a picturesque and accurate description of what took place before and after the victory over her people's foes.

The incident of the killing of Sisera, the scourge of Israel, related at the close of the fourth and fifth chapters, seems to be a blot on the narrative. If this account had been dressed up, it would not have had a place in it. The Bible writers, however, go on and tell things as they are. It may be said of this matter that there is no regret for the death of so cruel a man as Sisera with his long list of atrocities. It is the manner of his taking off by Jael. There can be no excuse offered for it. Only it may be said that in every war people seem to be beside themselves and do things that at other times they shrink in horror from. In the song of Deborah there is another version of the taking off of Sisera, in that Jael did what she did in front of him and not while he was asleep. But in those times, as in every war, the savage in man comes to the surface. We have to remember how long and how cruelly this people had suffered.

The Character of Deborah is marvelous in its combination of purely womanly qualities with the highest poetic art, faith in God and great executive ability.

Questions.—What can be said of the first woman leader of men in the Bible? Where are the deeds of Deborah recorded; what were her three problems? What can be said of the fear of the enemy? Describe Deborah and the three stages through which she probably passed. Give account of the strong arm methods decided upon; the joining of battle; the victory and the song of triumph. What can be said of the character of Deborah?

V

DELILAH

A TEMPTRESS

Delilah is a Type of "The Undesirable Woman." She is a wrecker wherever she is and she is in every community. In her we search in vain for any conscience in regard to what she does or any pity for her victims. Sometimes of great beauty and personal charm, she uses both for lures to do harm.

All her fascinations, and she has many, are exerted for the purpose of mutilating and destroying everything that is worth while in those upon whom she fixes her regard. These favoured and deluded ones are then cast out, with mocking laughter, to be scorned by all who pass by. The classic examples are Circe and The Sirens.

The Words and Deeds of this Woman are written in the Book of Judges. The account is short and to the point. It is completely set forth in eighteen verses—16:4-21. She lives in "The Valley of Sorek," the entrance to which is made very beautiful with rare flowers which perfume the air with sweet odours. The exit, then as now, is on "The Dread Desert of Dead Men's Bones." It goes by another name in our time, but the thing is the same.

Big Interests were Behind Delilah in getting Samson into "The Valley of Sorek." The Philistines did not want Samson around. He interfered with their evil practices. He was a champion of Israel. If this nation should come to the front then the Philistines who stood for all that was bad in government and morals must cease to be. Here was a reformer that must be got out of the way by any means that could be used.

Delilah Was Bribed. She was very willing to be bribed. Read the text—" And the lords af the Philistines came up unto her and said unto her, Entice him and see wherein his great strength lieth, and by what means we may prevail against him, that we may bind to afflict him: and we will give thee, every one of us eleven hundred pieces of silver "—Judges 16:5.

The Four Trials of the Wiles of Delilah. Note the systematic way in which this woman goes to work to wreck this strong man. She only makes four trials before she has him completely in her power. What a fool he is in the face of her power of cunning evil. She has no affection or passion for him while he is self-deluded into thinking she has.

It is the same old story through the ages. The methods of this woman, of this evil sort, remain unchanged. Samson thinks to make a fool of Delilah and he is the fool.

First—He declares, in answer to her entreaty to tell him the source of his strength, that if he is bound with seven green withes—16:7—his strength will go from him. (For withes read sinews, such as are used for bow strings.) Samson probably laughed, as he said this, but it is the woman who had the laugh on him. The sinews are easily torn apart.

Second—A test is made of new ropes. This fails—16:11.

Third—A test is made of weaving his hair in a web. This fails—16:13.

Fourth—A test is made of his " Nazarite Vow."—
16: 17. The end of poor Samson. He has come to
the point where he parts with his morality and spirituality and he is cast aside as a useless hulk. When
Delilah sees that he has told her the secret of his
power, she calls for the Philistines, who put out his
eyes, bind him with fetters of brass, and make him
to grind in their prison house. She goes seeking new
victims.

Every once in a while a big business man, a great
statesman or a learned professional man is lured
away into " The Valley of Sorek " and stripped
of his most precious possessions. The Philistines
and Delilah are still at work even in our times.

Why is this Story in the Bible?—It is not a
pleasant one. It is sordid to the last degree. A man
of great physical strength and with a keen mind is
beset, because he chooses to have it so, by a woman
of no morals. The reading of the result leaves a bad
taste in the mouth.

But the Bible would not be true to life and to its
mission if it did not hold up this mirror and let us
see the working out of this matter, told in restrained
language.

A Warning.—Here is a red flag that indicates
danger. It is bright coloured so that we may see it
and take care. No neutral color would do.

In New York harbour, where the ships of the
nations go in and out, there are bell buoys anchored
over rocks which approach the surface of the water.
The bells ring with every motion of the waves. They
speak no uncertain language. They cry continually
" Take care." " Keep away." " Come not here."

There are lighthouses all up and down the seacoast which send out great flashes of light to warn ships away. There are fog horns which, in foggy weather, bellow out hoarse shouts of caution.

A wise government sees that all possible means are used to keep ships and sailors in safety.

But after all precautions have been taken, no government can prevent ships or sailors from deliberately ignoring all the danger signals and going to destruction.

The dangers of life, as of the sea and seacoast, are real. Ignore them! Yes, if we care to, as Samson did. The result is the same.

A Temptress—Delilah.—"A" is used instead of "The" because she does not stand apart. She is one of a numerous class. To have her pointed out and described, as she is, is to indicate where the bed of quicksands is. Once step in and the quicksand does the rest.

Her Art is to Attract. No pains are spared. No trouble is too great. The Egyptian Potipher's wife stands beside her in her attempt upon Joseph. Jezebel, the wife of King Ahab, who tried to wreck Israel, is in the same class. The daughter of Herodias is not far away. The list is not a short one.

She Seeks to Find the Strength of her victims. She knows the weakness; this is as an open book; she does not bother here. "What is thy strength?" is her great question. A man may rise and conquer his weakness even at the moment of yielding or seeming to yield. His strength is always in reserve. It is a massive tower into which he may flee and be safe. But let a man once betray his strength and he has no reserve.

Her Purpose, Never Deviated From, is to wreck and destroy. All her brightness and glorious colouring are like those of the poison flowers.

Her Picture is in " The Gallery of The Proverbs." Look it up—

The Frame—" My son attend unto my wisdom and bow thine ear to my understanding: That thou mayest regard discretion, and that thy lips may keep knowledge "—Proverbs 5 : 1-2.

The Picture—" For the lips of a strange woman drop as a honeycomb, and her mouth is smoother than oil. But her end is bitter as wormwood, sharp as a two-edged sword. Her feet go down to death; her steps take hold on hell. Lest thou shouldest ponder the path of her life, her ways are movable that thou canst not know them. Hear me now therefore, O ye children, and depart not from the words of my mouth. Remove thy way far from her and come not nigh the door of her house : lest thou give thine honour unto others and thy years unto the cruel : Lest strangers be filled with thy wealth and thy labours be in the house of a stranger ; And thou mourn at the last, when thy flesh and thy body are consumed, And say, How have I hated instruction and my heart despised reproof ; And have not obeyed the voice of my teachers, nor inclined mine ear to them that instructed me ! "— Proverbs 5 : 3-13.

A Victim—Samson.—Again it is " A " instead of " The " because he does not stand apart but is one of a numerous class.

He Had a Good Start in Life. Read Judges, chapter 13. His parents were fine people. He was a " Promised " child to do a large and important work in delivering Israel from her oppressors. Nothing could have been fairer than this splendid beginning of the life of Samson. The vow of " The Nazarite " was to be his. His father and mother gave him every possible advantage. He had a splendid body and a keen, quick mind.

He Was Called to a Great and Honourable Office— to be a judge, ruler and deliverer of his people Israel.

His Choice Was to Set Aside the Advantages that came to him through his birth and calling. He seemed to do this deliberately. We have to conclude from such lives as that of this man, that everything does not hinge on birth, education and calling to a high position. It is a man's deliberate choice that counts largely in what he actually becomes.

He Was Willing to be Tempted. He put himself in the way of " A Temptress." Not once, but again and again. He went down to " The Valley of Sorek " to see Delilah. She did not seek him out. She sometimes does this.

He Crossed the Line Between Good and Evil several times and seemingly got back unharmed. He might have said to himself—" See how easy it is to cross this line and get back again. It is all nonsense about there being danger of being caught on the other side. With a man who has the great physical strength and keen mind I have, there is no bad situation from which I cannot escape. All this talk about evil harming anyone is old-fashioned."

He Was Caught on the Other Side of the Line by Delilah, just as she planned to catch him. She had her steel trap baited for him. He responded to the lure, just as many strong men, before and since him, have done. The jaws of the steel trap snapped shut and the victim could not get away. The cruel, big game huntress added one more scalp to her belt.

The End of a Victim. His eyes were put out. He was disgraced with fetters. He was made to grind in the prison house of his despised enemies. He was called for to make sport and be an object of derision. It is the same story to-day of men falling from high positions to be objects of sport.

We are told that Samson recovered his strength— Judges 16:22-31. But in his last feat of great strength, in the pulling down of the temple, we are told that he requested that he might die in order to be avenged for his two eyes that had been put out. Here was no moral purpose—Delilah seems to have killed that.

This story is left to make its own impression. There is no summing up. There is no moralizing. There is no preaching a sermon. The tale is sufficient in itself.

Questions.—What can be said of Delilah as a type? Where do we find the words and deeds of this woman? What big interests were behind Delilah; how was she bribed? What were the four trials of her wiles? Why is this story in the Bible; how is it a warning? What can be said of Delilah as a temptress? her art; what she sought; her purpose; her picture? What can be said of Samson, as a victim? his start in life; his call; his choice; his willingness to be tempted; his crossing the line between good and evil; how he was caught; his end?

VI

RUTH

A DEPENDABLE WOMAN

The Three Women, Ruth, Naomi and Orpah, whose lives are set forth in the Book of Ruth, are striking examples of what women did, in an age long passed away, under very distressful circumstances.

In our day women frequently have forced upon them similar conditions of life, hard to endure. The problems are old but presented under new and perplexing forms.

The question of " The Why of Difficulties? " is not easy to answer. The question of " How to Meet Difficulties? " has many solutions.

Each of the " Three Bible Women " took up her problem and attempted to solve it in a different way. How this was done, and why Ruth was accorded first place, is shown in what follows.

Ruth, a Dependable Woman.—Bereft of her husband, and without material resources of any kind, she faced the hard and bitter lot of a biting poverty. She felt it to be her duty to follow her mother-in-law, in a like sorry plight, into a new land and amongst an alien people.

The narrative is quite plain. Little is left to the imagination. The situation is gloomy. There is no hint of anything better in the future.

If Ruth shed any tears there is no record made of

the fact. She seems to have had no self-pity. She had no scorching words of blame for other people as some have, on account of her sad lot in life.

On the other hand there is a poise, a serenity and cheerfulness, about this woman which are remarkable. She does not pose as one who is doing anything remarkable. She just does the right thing in the most natural way.

When Naomi, her mother-in-law, seeks to dissuade her from going with her into new hardships, Ruth (read the first chapter of the book) declares—" Intreat me not to leave thee, or to return from following after thee: for whither thou goest I will go; and where thou lodgest I will lodge: thy people shall be my people, and thy God my God: where thou diest I will die, and there will I be buried: the Lord do so to me and more also, if ought but death part thee and me "—Ch. 1 : 16, 17.

She did a great favour to Naomi and she made it appear that it was Naomi that did her the favour. Ruth not only was able to carry her own heavy burden but assumed the burden of an older and weaker woman. She dealt not in words only, but deeds. In reading the narrative one is made to feel that here is a woman who is absolutely dependable when things are at the worst possible place. Here is a dependable independence of the right sort.

There is an " Independent Spirit " of the wrong sort abroad to-day, whereby some young women seek to repudiate all burdens which irk them in any way, and throw to the winds all obligations which seem to fetter them ; they declare they will live their own lives in their own way. This " Independent Spirit " once in, does what it pleases and it pleases not to do anything that would help any one else. It is absolutely indifferent to any misery it may cause. It seeks only its own pleasure.

It is refreshing to read the story of Ruth as one who cheerfully accepted responsibility, for those less able than herself. She gained her large place because of this.

Naomi, a Sensible Woman.—She lost her husband and two sons in a land foreign to her, and to which she had emigrated, when they were alive. She is without financial means.

Reading her story we are at once impressed with her common-sense way of sizing up the situation. There is no use to remain any longer in a place where there is little or nothing to be hoped for. Better get back to the place where she came from and where she is well known. She calls in her two daughters-in-law and explains the matter to them. She tells them how things stand and advises them to remain where they are and where they are well known. Here are no lamentations over what cannot be helped. All honour to Naomi, a sensible woman.

Orpah, an Emotional Woman.—She is in like condition with Ruth. She, however, looks at and takes matters very differently. She is very free with her demonstration of affection. She kisses her mother-in-law, doubtlessly, passionately. She is very fond of her, in her own way. She is greatly moved by the prospect of the parting of the ways. But that is all. She may go sobbing on her way back, but she goes.

She is of the " Emotional Type," very strong in expressions of affection and that is all. This type is found in many crises of family and church life. It expresses itself in good will and words, but for the lifting of any burden, or really helping to get things out of hard places, it is utterly useless.

Women of this sort may go a step further, and under pressure and stress of good feeling, promise any and all kinds of service, but when it comes to performance they turn back with Orpah.

The Book of Ruth consists of four short chapters. The first chapter is an account of Naomi and her two daughters and what they did when their home was broken up by the death of their husbands. The second, third and fourth chapters relate the courtship and marriage of Boaz and Ruth. At the conclusion of the last chapter there is given the lineage of King David and how he was related to Boaz and Ruth. Jesus Christ came through the royal line of David.

This book with that of Esther are the only two in the Bible named after women.

We have here a charming picture of pastoral life which we miss in the Book of Judges, which precedes it and that of Samuel, which follows it.

To read the Book of Judges, or even of Samuel, it would seem that people were always fighting. There are many valiant men but their deeds are deeds of blood. It is one war after another.

In Ruth there are no wars recorded. There are no battles mentioned. Here are good men and women engaged in peaceful pursuits. Here is a fertile valley, set between grim and stern mountains. There are flowers and fields, rich with waving grain, where every prospect pleases.

The Story is Simply Told.—It reads so easily that there is danger that its significance be lost. This is true of all really great tales.

Elimelech, his wife, Naomi, and their two sons, Mahlon and Chilion, in a time of famine, emigrate from Bethlehem to Moab. They sought better conditions. But in Moab they do not seem to have prospered. Elimelech died as did his two sons. The two sons, who had married in Moab, left Ruth and Orpah widows. What more natural than that Naomi should seek to return to Bethlehem, as she did. One daughter-in-law, Ruth, insisted on returning with her.

The Love of Ruth for Naomi is something unique. A like tale is not recorded anywhere in the literature of the world. There are abundance of examples of the love of a young woman for her parents, her brothers and sisters, of her lover, her husband, of friends of the same age, but that a young woman should profess such a strong and undying affection for her mother-in-law, a woman of maybe twice her age or more, is something entirely out of the ordinary. But there is not the slightest doubt that this affection existed in its purest and most unselfish form. Ruth's declaration of this love leaves no doubt of this—Ruth 1 : 15-18.

This picture is worth while looking at in its exaltation of a pure affection which begun without the slightest hope of any material reward but which was so abundantly rewarded. This account makes us think better of human nature. It lifts us up and exalts us.

It is totally unlike some modern tales that we read. For instance, the story of the talented young woman, anxious for an education and all that might come from it. Her mother, a widow, sympathized with her. She planned and schemed and went without that the daughter might have this education, but in doing this she grew worn and faded and wrinkled. The daughter was valedictorian of her class. She was ashamed of her mother's looks, acquired in her service, and determined that she should not come to the graduation exercises. But when the day came, the mother was there on the front seat, in an old, faded dress. The daughter, coming down from the platform, pretended not to see her mother and passed her by. Her name was not Ruth.

The Arrival in Bethlehem.—Everyone seems to have known Naomi before she left Bethlehem and when she returned "All the city was moved"— ch. 1:19. Everyone was naturally curious as to how she had prospered. When it was learned that she had come home, in sorrow and empty handed, there was an immediate falling off in interest. Then too, she had brought a daughter-in-law who had nothing. There might have been those who would have invited Naomi to lodge with them but they had no room for two. As long as her kinsfolk did not ask her to come and stay with them, she was too proud to go to them with a tale of her woes. It was a rather sad homecoming.

The Need of Food was very strong. What could be done about it? No one wanted any work done. All the occupations were filled. Ruth comes to the front as "A Dependable Woman." She

wasted no time over regrets in taking the step that
she did. She does not reproach Naomi for the total
lack of interest on the part of her friends and relatives. Yet if anything will make a man or woman
complain, and utter sharp words, it is the inability to
get food to eat.

Ruth notices that it is "The beginning of barley
harvest." She thinks a plan out by herself before she
proposes it to her mother-in-law. She will go and
glean after the reapers. She is not ashamed to take
her place with the sad, the poor and the outcast, for
of such were the gleaners. How did Ruth feel about
this matter of this low order of work? It is not recorded. But we are quite sure that she was not
ashamed of it. She did not make Naomi feel that
she was better out of the way. They talked of this
"Gleaning" as if it were the most natural thing in
the world and the right thing to do.

Courtship of Ruth. How naturally this thing
came about. Naomi knew all along who Boaz was,
in whose fields Ruth had chanced to go when she went
to glean. She did not tell Ruth. She was no match-
maker. Even when her daughter-in-law came home
with the news that she was gleaning in the fields of
Boaz, nothing was said about his being a near kinsman. It was Boaz, attracted by Ruth, who told her
that he knew all about her and of her kindness and
care for her mother-in-law. After this it was Naomi's
turn to tell Ruth about the kinship. This is a real
romance and a genuine love story. Read it for yourself. But and if Ruth had not been kind to Naomi,
when her fortunes were at the lowest ebb, no such
fortune would have been hers.

Marriage.—This is recorded in chapter 4: 13-22. This is one of the high places in the Old Testament.

Secret of Ruth's Getting On.—When any really great success in life is made there are always ample causes for it.

There are here, in Ruth:

1—*Ability to Decide for Right Things* when such a decision seems to involve great hardships.

2—*Adherence to Such a Decision* under continued adverse circumstances.

3—*Making Another Person Feel that You Can be Depended Upon.*

4—*Unselfish Love* and willingness to suffer and work for another less fortunately situated.

5—*Great Faith* in God and humanity.

Questions.—What can be said of the three women of the Book of Ruth? Ruth, a dependable woman? Naomi, a sensible woman? Orpah, an emotional woman? Give an account of the Book of Ruth. How is the story simply told? Describe the love of Ruth for Naomi. Give an account of the arrival in Bethlehem. What of the need of food? What of the courtship and marriage of Ruth? Give five points in the secret of Ruth's getting on.

VII

HANNAH

MOTHER OF A GREAT PROPHET

The Advent of Hannah marks an exceedingly favourable turning point in the affairs of the Israelites. A central government is set up. The loosely associated tribes become a strong and vigorous nation.

Samuel, the son of Hannah, was the leader in this betterment movement. His brilliant and well deserved fame is apt to throw a shadow upon the greatness of Hannah which we desire to show, without this shadow, in this study.

The Bible, in comparatively few instances, gives us the early childhood history of its heroes, but in the case of Samuel it is given in full.

Hannah in the first two chapters of the First Book of Samuel is accorded all credit for what she did in the training of her great son for the splendid task which he accomplished in the face of what seemed, at the time, insurmountable difficulties.

She is No Subordinate or Weak Character. She knows just exactly what she wants. She prays for a son. A son is born to her.

She knows what she wants her son to do. She sets his feet in the path of what he afterwards did with such success.

She does not allow him to grow up anyway and anyhow, but plans his training in accordance with what are now considered the most advanced and scientific methods of child culture.

Hannah, in Some Respects, is Greater than Samuel. Elkanah, her husband, does not seem to have been in sympathy with her. Her environment was not favorable. She had to break away from old traditions and blaze a new trail.

The Old Order of Things, when the first book of Samuel opens, was bad; about as bad as it could be. Since the death of Joshua and all through the period of the time described in the Book of The Judges, things seemed to be deteriorating and going from bad to worse. Instead of drawing together the tribes were getting farther apart. They were lapsing from the high standards of morality and spirituality, set up by Moses in the " Ten Commandments," into the loose ways of the idolatrous peoples about them. The high priest, Eli, was a good but weak old man. His sons had no regard for their religious office or even common decency. They scorned their father and his advice and exhortations—Ch. 2: 12-17 and 22-25. The end seemed in sight when the " Chosen Nation " would cease to function as " The People of Jehovah."

The New Order of Things and how it was brought about is told in the First and Second Books of Samuel. Instead of sporadic attempts at reform, as in the Book of Judges, Hannah is chosen and she trains Samuel, from his earliest infancy, for his task. It is a new method, the long way around, but it worked. When the record is finished, everything is changed for the better. There is no longer any question as to the survival of Israel. Hannah takes her seat amongst " The Mighty Ones," appointed to do a work for her people which is unique.

Place of Hannah.—She had a strong personality and an important mission. She did not have the independence of Miriam, the ability to lead men like Deborah or the decision of Ruth. She worked on an entirely different line. If you had lived, when she did, and had met her some day when she was going to the temple to see her son, you might have had the impression that she was a quiet home body with nothing remarkable about her. If you had talked with her, the impression would not probably have been altered. Her mission had not then come to its flowering time, as we see it now.

Claim to Fame.—It is a large one. Her portrait occupies a conspicuous place in the Bible Gallery which is " The World's Gallery of Lasting Fame " for men and women who have done the very greatest things.

She Trained and Inspired Another Soul to do that which she did not feel that she was capable of doing. She subordinated herself to this work with a wholehearted enthusiasm. In placing her boy in the temple, that he might have a better opportunity to be trained, she put aside her mother feelings and desires. For the most part, people who find that they cannot carry out their plans to do what they want to do, give up and lapse back into doing nothing. Hannah had a new conception of life and its possibilities in the life of her son. She sought to inspire him with her high ideals, hopes and aspirations. How effectively she did this is shown by the record.

Culture of a Child.—We, in our day, are coming to recognize the possibilities in a child and the necessity of bringing them out by the proper training. This cannot be done by haphazard methods. It is painstaking, careful work. We now have many books on this subject. Schools with trained teachers abound. Hannah had no books but she seems to have anticipated, in her treatment of Samuel, all that is worth while in the modern methods and successfully used them.

Grasp of the Future.—Hannah had a wide and far-seeing vision of what she wanted Samuel to become. She did not look forward to ten or twenty or forty or fifty years of service but longer. She said when she brought him to the temple—Ch. 1: 27, 28—" For this child I prayed; and the Lord hath given me my petition, which I asked of him: Therefore also I have lent him to the Lord; as long as he liveth he shall be lent to the Lord." She knew the sore need of her people. She had seen temporary leaders come and go, do a little work, and leave things much as they were before. It is comparatively easy to get people to undertake things that are limited in their scope to a few months or possibly years, but to enlist for a lifetime service—that is different. All honour to Hannah, who, home body that she was, had this vision of a far-reaching lifetime service. It is this forelook which the Bible urges upon every one.

Personal Characteristics.—These are many. Let us consider a few of them.

Poetess of No Mean Rank. Her song, recorded in First Samuel 2: 1-10, shows poetical ability of the highest order. It is fully equal to any of the Psalms of David. Here God's attributes of power, holiness, knowledge, majesty and purity are wonderfully set forth. Confidence in God is urged, without which there can be no stable belief in anything or any incentive to work.

Prophetess—Ch. 2:9, 10. Hannah shows her grasp of the future in these two verses. She has seen the plan of things and her soul is satisfied.

Spiritual. She moves and has her being in accord with God.

A Good Mother. This goes without comment. Every line of what is written about her life breathes of her love and care for her son.

Work Through Samuel.—No man ever did a larger or greater work for his country. When he came to manhood, after his training by his mother, and his call by God—Ch. 3—he found Israel disrupted at home and despised abroad.

He changed everything for the better without violent or revolutionary methods. He was quiet and calm but exceedingly effective in all that he did.

1—*Samuel Responded to the Care and Culture Bestowed Upon Him by His Mother.* There never seems to have been any departure from the lines laid down for him by her.

2—*He Was the Last One of the Judges and One of the First Ones of the Prophetic Order.* This was a new order separate from the priesthood. Up to this time the priest has been the chosen one through whom God communicated His will to His people. Now the prophet to a large extent takes his place. He represented the independence of the moral portion of the people as distinct from government or priestly enactment.

Schools were established in which prophets were trained for their work much like our theological seminaries.

Instruction was given in the Sacred Books and in poetry. The pupils were taught to play upon musical instruments.

The results were far-reaching. The graduates of these schools became teachers of religion and of patriotism. They made copies of The Sacred Law and kept the text free from error. They became the preachers to the people. They denounced national, family and individual sins. They encouraged the people in times of trial and disaster. Some, but not all, possessed and exercised prophetic gifts. The prophets had much to do with the raising of the standards of morality and spirituality.

3—*Founder of the Israelitish Monarchy.* It is plainly evident that God intended this nation to live directly under His own guidance and care. But it did not seem capable of living up to this high ideal. When the people asked for a king, Samuel was directed to grant their request.

He anointed two kings, in succession, over the nation. First, Saul—Ch. 10—and second, David—Ch. 16. Saul proved unworthy of the post and was removed from his high office. David proved wholly worthy of the trust reposed in him and, under him, great glory and power came to this people.

4—*He Was a Man with Clean Hands. He Prided Himself Upon His Integrity*—Ch. 12:1-5. He regarded public office as a public trust. When he resigned his leadership of Israel after he had anointed Saul king, in laying down his office, " Samuel said unto all Israel, Behold I have hearkened unto your voice in all that ye said unto me and have made a king over you. And now behold the king walketh before you: and I am old and greyheaded; and behold my sons are with you: and I have walked before you from my childhood unto this day. Behold here I am, witness against me before the Lord, and before his anointed: whose ox have I taken? or whose ass have I taken? or whom have I defrauded? whom have I oppressed? or of whose hand have I received any bribe to blind mine eyes therewith? and I will restore it to you." What more could Samuel say? What greater appeal could he make? Few men at the close of such a public career as Samuel had would dare to say what he did, because it could not be said with truth.

5—*The People Applauded Samuel's Address* and said—" Thou hast not defrauded us or oppressed us, neither hast thou taken ought of any man's hand." Taken all in all, there is no greater figure in the history of Israel.

The Appreciation of Hannah, who lives in the fame of her prophet son, cannot be too great.

Questions.—What can be said of the advent of Hannah? What about her character? How is she, in some respects, greater than Samuel? What can be said of the old order of things? How was the new order brought about? What is the place of Hannah? What is her claim to fame? The culture of her child? What was Hannah's grasp of the future? Give her personal characteristics. What was her work through Samuel? Name the five points.

VIII

THE QUEEN OF SHEBA

THE SEEKER AFTER WISDOM

The Desire for Knowledge.—In our "Studies of Famous Bible Women" we come now to a new type—"The Seeker After Wisdom."

If we judge from the large and increasing numbers of young women enrolling in our institutions of learning, and their eagerness in the pursuit of knowledge, we might say that this is a purely modern development.

But, in this matter, the Queen of Sheba was certainly a pioneer. She undertook a long and tedious journey, at a fabulous cost, in order that she might increase her stock of knowledge. On her part, no effort was too great, and no price too high, in order that she might pass through the inner doors to a higher wisdom.

The Queen of Sheba—the Pupil.

She is credited with being the ruler of the Great Kingdom of Southern Arabia. What we know of her life, so far as the Bible is concerned, is written in ten verses of the tenth chapter of the Book of I Kings, and a parallel account in II Chronicles 9: 1-12.

Outside the Bible there are endless tales of her beauty of person, power, and royal magnificence. But the Scriptural account is so well written, so enlightening, that it has given to her a world-wide undying fame. Who is there who does not know of this young queen who came up from the South " To Jerusalem with a very great train, with camels that bare spices, and very much gold, and precious stones?" Of the hardships of the journey, the long nights and weary days of slow travel, nothing is recorded, for they would not be worthy to be considered in such a quest for the higher learning.

King Solomon—the Teacher.

Third King of the Israelitish Kingdom. He succeeded his father, David, who had been a mighty man in his day, consolidated the tribes, and ruled over a united and prosperous people from his capitol, the city of Jerusalem. Never were the prospects brighter for a nation, than when Solomon took his place on the throne.

A Great Builder. The account of these building operations is found in I Kings, chapters six to ten, inclusive. He was seven years in constrncting a " House of God " or what is known as " Solomon's Temple," one of the wonders of the world in its time. Gold and silver were used here as base metal is used elsewhere. He was thirteen years in building his own palace and in practically remaking the city with new streets, walls, and public service edifices. In the dazzling beauty of these new architectural creations, Solomon held his court.

A Mighty Ruler. He strengthened his kingdom at home and made alliances with the nations round about.

The Wise Man, " The Wisest Man of the East." As such he was known throughout his world. His fame traveled far. The source of his wisdom is set down in the third chapter of I Kings. It is related that when God asked him his chief request, in the beginning of his rule, that Solomon desired " Wisdom " above everything—" Give therefore thy servant an understanding heart to judge thy people, that I may discern between good and bad: for who is able to judge this, thy so great a people? "—I Kings 3 : 9.

The Visit of the Royal Pupil to the Royal Teacher.—Great preparations must have been made upon both sides. Embassies must have been sent up from the South to Jerusalem to see if such a visit would be welcome. After the embassies had completed their work then came the task of making ready the caravan and getting together the gifts to be presented, or the tuition fees. Equal preparations must have been made on the part of Solomon to receive so great a company into his city, his college.

What the Queen of Sheba did not Come For.—It was not a visit of state, or to make a new treaty of any sort or kind. It was not to behold solely the magnificence of the court of Solomon, although it was great. It was not to gaze upon the fine buildings of Jerusalem. If the Queen of Sheba had desired to do any of these things she could have done them to much better advantage in Egypt or gone on further to Nineveh or Babylon, where things were on a much grander scale than even Solomon could offer. Her court was no small thing.

The Real Purpose of the Visit.—Of this we are not left in the slightest doubt. The narrative is very explicit—" She came to prove him (Solomon) with hard questions "—I Kings 10: 1. She was insatiable in her desire for knowledge.

She was of that class of young women who, entering college halls, delight the professors with their eagerness to master the subjects presented in the classrooms.

She asked a thousand and one questions " And Solomon told her all her questions: there was not anything hid from the king that he told her not "— I Kings 10: 3.

Of these questions and answers there are many accounts in the literature of the East.

Here is something to be considered by those who think that the Bible is only concerned with religious matters and has no concern with those that interest the mind. Both are set forth.

Here was a college for young women, with one teacher and one pupil, but both made up in eagerness to receive and impart learning with any institution of learning that has a thousand students and many teachers.

The Queen of Sheba asked questions and received replies until she was satisfied and "There was no more spirit in her." She said to the king—" It was a true report that I heard in mine own land of thy acts and thy wisdom"—I Kings 10: 6.

The Wisdom Sought embraced all the subjects upon which men cannot help thinking. If we turn to " The Wisdom Literature of The Bible " we will see how these subjects are treated.

The Book of Proverbs is one of the books of wisdom. It will serve as an example of some of the things which were brought up between the Queen of Sheba and Solomon.

It Begins as Follows—The introduction is short and to the point. " The proverbs of Solomon, the

son of David, the king of Israel. To know wisdom
and instruction; to perceive the words of understanding: To receive the instruction of wisdom, justice and
judgment and equity; To give subtilty to the simple,
to the young man knowledge and discretion. A wise
man will hear and will increase learning; and a man
of understanding shall attain unto wise counsels.
To understand a proverb and the interpretation; the
words of the wise and their dark sayings. The fear
of the Lord is the beginning of knowledge: but fools
despise wisdom and instruction. My son hear the
instruction of thy father, and forsake not the law of
thy mother: For they shall be an ornament of grace
upon thy head, and chains about thy neck. My son
if sinners entice thee consent thou not. If they say,
Come with us, let us lay wait for blood, let us lurk
privily for the innocent without cause: Let us swal-
low them up alive as the grave; and whole as those
that go down into the pit. . . . My son, walk not thou
in the way with them; refrain thy foot from their
path. . . . Wisdom crieth without; she uttereth her
voice in the streets. She crieth, in the chief place of
concourse, in the openings of the gates: in the city,
saying, How long, ye simple ones, will ye love simplicity? And the scorners delight in their scorning,
and fools hate knowledge?"—Proverbs, first chapter.

*There Are Two Voices and Two Ways Set Forth
in this Book.*

The first voice utters words of wisdom, understanding, knowledge, prudence, instruction and
discretion.

The second voice utters words of folly, simplicity,
brutishness, stupidity, ignorance and villainy.

Wisdom is personified. She utters her voice in

the broad places, at the head of noisy streets. The simple pay no heed. They fall into the trap set for their feet.

Folly also utters her invitation in the same places. " Whoso is simple, let him turn in hither where stolen waters are sweet and forbidden fruit is tempting " but " her guests are in the depths of hell." Note the graphic picture painted in chapters eight and nine. The problem is up to everyone as to which voice he will heed and in what way he will walk.

A Strong Feature of this wisdom literature is that it will not admit of any conflict between the world of nature and God. Religion here is good sense, mastery of affairs, a well furnished intellect and the best means for the highest ends. To the Hebrew mind, God is in every event. His presence is near. His care is over all. There are not two worlds but one. Not two lives but one. There is not a question that is not here discussed—Who is God? What is man? What is our purpose in the world? What is good sense in business? How make the most of life?

The Purpose of the Book is practical. It is to instruct everyone reading it so that the very utmost success can be attained in life. Here are good, wise, witty, sarcastic, helpful, scornful, stinging, upbuilding proverbs but every one is framed to keep us on the right, and turn our feet from the wrong road.

It is Divided into Seven Parts. Each part distinct in itself and well worth the most careful study.

1—The Praise of Wisdom. Chapters 1-9. The speaker addresses the reader as, " My Son." The benefits and greatness of wisdom are shown.

2—The Proverbs of Solomon. Chapters 10 to

22: 16. A large number of wise sayings with no common topic.

3—The Sayings of the Wise. Chapter 22: 17 to 24th chapter. No common topic. Proverbs by different authors.

4—A Collection of Solomon's Proverbs. Chapters 25 to 29. Some of the oldest and best of " The Wise King's Sayings." Well worth study.

5—The Words of Agur. Chapter 30. This is a sermon prophecy rather than a set of proverbs. He deals with a topic which seems to be beyond him.

6—The Words of King Lemuel. Chapter 31 : 1-9. The duty of kings.

7—An Acrostic Poem. Chapter 31: 10-31. In praise of a woman who is a good wife, home maker, and business woman.

The Proverbs for Study, if there is only limited time, should be the ones in chapters 25 to 29, inclusive, of King Solomon.

Questions.—What can be said of the desire for knowledge? How was the Queen of Sheba a pioneer? Give some account of the queen. Give some account of King Solomon as a great builder, mighty ruler and wise man. What can be said of the visit of the royal pupil to the royal teacher? What did the queen not come for? What was the real purpose of the visit? Of what did the wisdom sought consist? What can be said of the Book of Proverbs, how does it begin, what of the two voices and the two ways, the strong feature, the purpose, how is it divided, of what do the different sections treat?

IX

THE WIDOW OF ZAREPHATH

FAITH UNDER DIFFICULTIES

The Story of the Widow of Zarephath is an incident in the career of the prophet Elijah. It is told in full in I Kings 17: 8-24. There are only seventeen short verses. They are filled with an intense human interest.

The fiery reformer, Elijah, suddenly comes upon the scene of action—I Kings 17: 1—to proclaim a famine, of several years' duration, on account of the evil course of Ahab, king of Israel—I Kings 16: 28-34.

While waiting for the end of the famine, the prophet is fed by " The Widow of Zarephath." The place is thought to be the modern Sarafend, about thirteen miles north of Tyre, on the spur of the mountain which divides the plain of Tyre from that of Sidon.

Facing a Hard Situation.—Poverty of any kind is not easy to bear. But that of " The Widow," at this time, was a biting one. It was removed only one step from utter destitution and starvation. Her ordinary resources were meager, at the best, but now they were so lowered that she could not look forward to any prospest for to-morrow, after to-day's scanty supply of food had been eaten. Her neighbours might not have been much better off.

A Singular Request. When therefore the prophet

Elijah appears before her, asking to share her little bit of food, she must have been very much surprised. We have to remember that she did not know about "The Prophet" as we do. He came to her as a travel-stained and worn old man, with long hair and beard. He says nothing about who he is or the nature of his mission. He asks first for a drink of water. As she went to get it "He called to her and said, Bring me, I pray thee, a morsel of bread in thine hand"—I Kings 17:11.

The Astonishment of the Woman at this Request is reflected in the narrative. It doubtless seemed to her that he ought to know the condition of things in this famine time. Why, she said—"As the Lord thy God liveth, I have not a cake, but a handful of meal in a barrel, and a little oil in a cruse: and, behold, I am gathering two sticks, that I may go in and dress it for me and my son, that we may eat it and die"— I Kings 17:12.

This Woman Faces Her Trouble. She blames no one. She is self-respecting in her dire need. She does not rail at anything or anybody about the injustice of things. She does not mention anything about the inequalities of life. She does nothing about organizing a mob to raid the shops for the necessities of life as has been so often done when hunger presses beyond a certain point.

Courage, of the rarest kind, is manifested. We marvel at the pluck of "The Widow of Zarephath," whose name is withheld from us. It is comparatively easy to have courage when there is something tangible to fight, but the slow approach of starvation is intangible, and who can fight it? It ordinarily calls out the meanest and bitterest things in the heart of man. A celebrated English novelist once wrote—" It is only by the candle held in the skeleton hand of poverty, that a man can see his own dark heart." History has again and again illustrated the truth of what he has said. But here is the rare exception.

" The Candle of Poverty," which lights up the soul of this woman, finds no bitterness, no sourness, no dark railings against fate, no comparisons of her evil lot with the good lot of others. We see here, a fine courage.

Kindness.—With what bitter scorn " The Widow " might have answered the request of Elijah for food! She might have asked him what he expected in this famine-stricken land! She might have poured out upon him the vials of her wrath. She might have bidden him " To get along on his way and ask where people were able to give rather than to take the last morsel of food out of her mouth."

She did none of these things. Notice the kindliness of her manner. She would gladly help if she could, but the puzzle to her is, how is she going to do anything. Turning the whole thing over in her mind, she seems to resolve to put the whole thing up to this old man who is asking " Impossibilities." She has only a little meal and a little oil to make a small cake for herself and her son. Now, if he were in her place, what would he do? She did not want to withhold anything. She wants to be kind. But here are the facts in the case. What can best be done? What more royal spirit ever dwelt in the heart of a woman than this?

First Trial of Faith.—The Jews have a saying—" When the tale of bricks is doubled then comes Moses." This was a dark hour in the life of this woman.

What must have been the perplexity of the woman, after she had stated her case, to have the prophet tell her to go ahead with her baking and to use up the meal and the oil and to serve him first. " Serve him first "—yes, that was what he said. To be sure the man said that " The Lord God of Israel saith, The barrel of meal shall not waste, neither shall the cruse of oil fail, until the day that the Lord sendeth rain upon the earth." But how was she to know that this man spoke rightly? Suppose she did as directed and the promise did not come true? What could be done about it? Nothing, nothing at all. She and her son would starve to-day and not to-morrow. The decision had to be made.

Then as now—" Faith is the substance of things hoped for, the evidence of things not seen." There always has to be a venture. The woman made the venture and the words of the prophet came true— " And the barrel of meal wasted not, neither did the cruse of oil fail." She and her son did not die on the morrow as she feared. They lived because of her faith.

This is an old story but its teaching is as true to-day as it was in the long past. We must venture be-fore we can have the things we desire. This woman was offered a partnership with God. What an offer it was! The same offer is made to-day to every one to share our substance with God, on the same terms. What will we do with the offer?

The Reward of Faith and Hospitality. It must

have been a great surprise to this woman to find that the plan worked. However much she might have hoped that the plan would work she could not be certain. Her courage, her kindliness, her faith and her self-respect, all helped along, This was good ground. We are taught and are slowly coming to believe that anger, hatred and kindred things, cherished and exercised, will do us personal physical, mental, and moral harm. Why not believe that the virtues, as exercised by this woman, will do equal good?

If this woman had let come into her heart all the evil things that clamoured to come in, when she was at her darkest hour, there would have been no chance for her faith to be exercised. All honour to " The Widow of Zarephath," who would not be downed by her great trials.

She showed a great hospitality when it seemed as if that would hurt both herself and her son. It is small wonder that she is given such large a place amongst the women of the Bible.

The Second Trial of Faith.—The first has been passed. The second is now at hand. What is it? Why should she not rest from her labours? All things seemed to be going well until one day " The Widow's Son " is taken sick. " And his sickness was so sore that there was no breath left in him." This woman's heart is torn with an anguish unspeakable. She, who could face starvation with her son, cannot bear to face his death alone. What shall she do? What can she do? This is indeed a trial!

But now she knows what to do and where to go. In the first trial she was stoical, to a certain degree. The source of help approached her. Elijah laid before her his proposition. In this second trial she shows that she has learned where to go to receive help. This is a great advance.

But let us not suppose that this woman is not human. She approaches Elijah with blame for him and blame for herself. This is most natural. She thinks that she has done something, has sinned in some way, and that the death of her son is the punishment for it. She connects " This Man of God," as she has come to regard him, with the penalty.

This experience of having people blame themselves for sins of omission and commission, when their loved ones die, is a most common one to ministers, when, in fact, they are blameless. As for Elijah, he says nothing when the woman accuses him of a part in the penalty. He is also very human in his sympathy. He knows that this woman is beside herself with her grief, has done nothing evil and knows not what she is saying. Therefore he says nothing in return but what can be of help. He takes the boy and he is restored to his mother.

The Vindication of Faith. Here is a higher step taken. Faith was rewarded in the first trial. Here, in the second, it is vindicated. The two trials have been searching to the last degree and the woman has come out from them conscious that her faith is on firm ground—I Kings 17: 24.

In Conclusion. In studying the career of Elijah, of which this study is but an incident, we deal with matters of kings and queens and the affairs of nations. Things are on a large scale. It might well be said of most of us that we are not living on a big scale. Hence such stories, as that of " The Widow of Zarephath," are, we think, put in that we may see that as God deals with " The Greater Ones " in life so He deals with " The Lesser Ones." The situations and experiences are not far-fetched but those which are constantly recurring in different forms.

Questions.—What can be said of the story of the widow of Zarephath? What about this woman facing a hard situation? What was the singular request of Elijah? The astonishment of the woman? What of " The Widow's " courage and kindliness? What was the first trial of faith and its reward? The second trial of faith and its vindication? What can be said in conclusion?

X

JEZEBEL

THE RUTHLESS QUEEN

The Name—Jezebel.—What is in a name? Sometimes much and sometimes nothing at all. In this case it has become so packed with evil significance that no mother would think of naming her girl baby, " Jezebel." To call any woman " A Jezebel " would be equivalent to offering her a gross insult.

A World-Wide Bad Reputation.—How did this woman get this unsavory renown? It is an interesting study. The story extends over many years. It is all dark without a single light spot. It is told, in detail, from her marriage to Ahab, king of Israel, to her ignominious death—I Kings 16: 31 to II Kings 9: 31-37. She pursued her reckless course, in spite of checks and warnings, to the bitter end. After the custom of the Scriptures there is little or no comment, only the facts are stated and left to make their own impression.

Daughter of Ethbaal—King of the Zidonians.— Outwardly the Zidonians were great. They administered large affairs. They had and displayed much wealth. In character they were cruel and rapacious. They stopped at nothing to carry out their purposes. The worship was that of Baal and Astarte in which at times, human sacrifices were offered and licentious practices were common. They catered to the lowest and basest instincts in human nature. They recognized no morality or virtue as we know them. The Zidonians had no use whatever for the religion of Jehovah with its "Ten Commandments" and its "Purities" and "Moralities." They were not straightened in what they did by any considerations of the rights of any one so long as they had the power to crush all opposition. They rode rough shod over the weak and helpless. The king ruled by might and his will and word were absolute.

The Princess, Jezebel, was like her father and her people in all their characterictics. What more natural than that she should be? As a young and headstrong woman she might have accentuated them.

Wife of Ahab—The King of Israel.—He was the seventh in line, after Solomon, in the divided kingdom. It was the policy of Jeroboam, the first king after Solomon, to try to win the Israelites away from the worship of Jehovah in order that they might not unite with the kingdom of Judah in Jerusalem. Ahab, when he came to the throne, entered heartily into the policy of Jeroboam to win the Israelites from the religion of their fathers—I Kings 16: 30-33.

In Marrying Jezebel Ahab found an able helper, who proposed not to be troubled by any scruples whatsoever in rooting up and destroying the old religion of Israel. In this she would take a perfect delight. As queen, with absolute power, her opportunities to work her will, would be unlimited. She took advantage of every one of them. Aided and abetted by his wife "Ahab did more to provoke the Lord God of Israel to anger than all the kings of Israel that were before him"—I Kings 16: 33.

An Apt Pupil in Evil.—It might be said of

Jezebel that she was a product of the court in which she was brought up and of the condition of affairs in which she found herself in the Israelitish court, after her marriage. Much might be said with truth, along this line. But the fact is that this woman was no weakling. She had a mind of her own. Strong as Ahab was, she dominated him again and again. She took charge of situation after situation to make it bend to her will. She became what she did because that was what she desired to be. She resisted any influence to which she did not wish to yield.

A Strong and Cruel Personality.—No one can deny the strength of the personality of Jezebel. She was self-centered. She asked no advice and cared for none in making up her mind and carrying out her plans. Others must bow to her ways, not she to them. In this she was a true Zidonian.

She was ruthless in what she did without the slightest compunction of conscience. She was more like some huge machine, rolling along a road, maiming and killing people, without stopping for anything until it reached its destination.

She banished and killed the prophets of Jehovah. She tore down His altars and set up the altars and images of Baal and Astarte with their inhuman and licentious orgies.

The Attempt to Kill the Prophet Elijah —I Kings 19:2. The whole story ought to be read as it is set down in I Kings 17:1 to 19:18. It begins with an account of the attempt to bring Ahab and Jezebel to their senses in what they were doing to destroy the old religion of Jehovah.

After expostulation and warnings have been exhausted, a three years' famine is proclaimed by Elijah. But the warning is unheeded by Ahab and Jezebel and the three years' drought seems not to be cared for in any way.

Then Elijah calls for a test as to—" Who is God?" Let him answer by fire, in consuming a sacrifice. This test is made in the open air on Mt. Carmel. The prophets of Baal, a great number of them, call all day on Baal to answer by fire, in the consumption of their sacrifice but they get no answer. When the evening comes on, Elijah alone calls on Jehovah, who answers by fire, at once consuming the sacrifice. Then Elijah predicts the breaking of the drought which comes to pass with an abundance of rain. Ahab is convinced of the power of Jehovah, as are the people.

Jezebel is unconvinced by this mighty display of Jehovah's power and greatness. She is only contemptuous and angry. Instead of being overawed, she is defiant. Is she afraid? Not so. This is an attitude characteristic of this woman. It is what might be expected. She goes further.

Jezebel Threatens the Prophet Who Escapes Her. She will show her contempt. She sends a " Messenger unto Elijah, saying, So let the gods do to me, and more also, if I make not thy life as one of them (referring to the Baal prophets who died on Mt. Carmel), by to-morrow about this time "—I Kings 19 : 2. It is not her fault that she did not slay Elijah.

The futility of attempting to convince those who do not want to be convinced, of the greatness of Jehovah and the glory of purity and righteousness, is set forth in the experience of Elijah when he fled from Jezebel into the wilderness and was utterly discouraged. The Lord, it is shown, may not be in the strong wind, the great earthquake, but in " A still, small voice." Read I Kings 19:9-12.

Jesus Christ calls attention to this matter when He declares that those who do not want to believe will not be " Persuaded, though one rose from the dead "—Luke 16: 30, 31. That God is perfectly able to take care of His interests is shown in the instructions given to Elijah to anoint Jehu, in place of Ahab, king of Israel—I Kings 19: 13-18. Ahab and Jezebel are declared to be dethroned. The decree has gone forth, soon to be executed.

The Cold-Blooded Murder of Naboth, to steal his vineyard. Here the real character of Jezebel comes out in its unmistakable colours. The whole story is told in the twenty-first chapter of the First Book of Kings. Ahab had a palace at Jezreel which city was on the border of the tribe of Issacher. Near by Naboth had a vineyard. The king wanted it. He offered to buy it or give another place in exchange. But as it had belonged in Naboth's family for a good while, he did not want to sell it. Ahab felt so badly about it that he refused food. His wife, Jezebel, finding out what was the matter, declared that she could not see, if he was king, why the matter could not be easily settled. She took charge of the affair.

Notice her deliberate cunning. She wrote letters to the elders of the city, in the king's name, sealing them with his seal. These letters directed that a fast be proclaimed and that Naboth be set on high amongst the people, but at the very moment of his triumph, he should be accused of blasphemy against his God and his king by two false witnesses and that he should be stoned to death.

The Diabolical Plan was Carried Out to the bitter end. Then Jezebel, having caused Naboth to be murdered, came to Ahab and told him to go in and take possession. There is not the slightest expression of regret at what she has done.

For a little time, all seems to go well. Ahab expresses no sorrow when he hears that Naboth has been killed. He goes down to take possession of his vineyard.

The Dooms Pronounced Upon Ahab and Jezebel.—There is no doubt of the dominance of Jezebel over Ahab. She is the stronger personality. It was said of him—I Kings 21 : 25—" There was none like Ahab who did sell himself to work wickedness in the sight of the Lord whom Jezebel, his wife, stirred up."

But wait! Is Ahab going to enter into what Jezebel has got for him by the murder of Naboth? It looks that way but it does not turn out that way. Elijah, who fled before Jezebel, has returned and meets him. There is here no calling down of fire from heaven but a setting before Ahab of his sins and his doom. Of Jezebel, the queen, the prophet predicts her death. It is not a pleasant thing to think about, that " The dogs shall eat Jezebel by the wall of Jezreel." Read about it in I Kings 21 : 15-26.

When Ahab heard the " Dooms " pronounced, he humbled himself and repeated—I Kings 21 : 27-29—but there was no turning back on the part of Jezebel.

The Ignominious Death of Jezebel.—What a

word picture of that we are given in II Kings 9: 30-37. It is difficult to look at and consider in its awful details. It revolts our feelings. But it is of a piece with what she has been doing to others all her life.

She was arrogant, vain, proud, cruel, sarcastic and mean to the last. She is in Jezreel when she hears of the coming of Jehu, the new king. She paints her face and arranges her hair to be attractive once more and looks out of the window. As she sees Jehu she sarcastically inquires—" Had Zimri peace who slew his master?" Jehu looks up and inquiring, " Who is on his side?" orders her to be thrown down. Then was this arrogant, cruel queen humbled in the dust, who had never humbled herself in any way to any one, but always rode rough shod over everyone who disputed her will. Jehu remembered when he came in that she was a king's daughter, and ordered her buried, but they found only the remnants, after the dogs had done with her.

Questions.—What can be said of the name—Jezebel? Give some account of her as the daughter of Ethbaal, king of the Zidonians. Was the princess like her father and people? What can be said about her as the wife of Ahab? What did he find in Jezebel? Was she an apt pupil in evil? What can be said about her personality? Describe her relations with Elijah and her attempt to kill him. Give the account of Jezebel's cold-blooded murder of Naboth. Tell something of the " Dooms " pronounced upon Ahab and Jezebel. Describe the ignominious death of Jezebel.

XI

ESTHER

SELF-SACRIFICE FOR A CAUSE

Esther is the Heroine of the book which bears her name.

From the condition of an orphan, in the humble home of her cousin, Mordecai, she rose to be the queen of one of the world's greatest empires.

After she became queen, she voluntarily placed her life in jeopardy in order that she might save her people from massacre. She is a striking example of a woman, who having everything, was willing to renounce all for a great cause.

She is honoured not only by having a Bible book named after her but also in having her splendid act of renunciation and self-sacrifice commemorated in the yearly " Purim Festival " even to our own time.

What She Did, and how she did it, is told in ten intensely interesting chapters.

The Scene is laid in far-off Persia. It is in the palace of Ahasuerus, " Who reigned, from India even unto Ethiopia, over a hundred and seven and twenty provinces "—Esther 1: 1.

A vast realm governed by a single despotic ruler, from a central city, with none of the modern means of communication and transportation which seem to us so essential to keep a nation one and in order,

The palace was a huge magnificent building, furnished with oriental extravagance and luxury.

There are Five Principal Characters.—They

are named in the order in which they appear in the book.

Ahasuerus, who is supposed to be Xerxes, a voluptuous and despotic ruler. While his will is absolute, he seems at times to be worked as a puppet by those who can manage to get hold of the controlling strings.

History represents him as mighty and at the same time dissolute, vengeful and vain, but not without intelligence and a certain sense of justice and generosity. But what could be expected of a man with such unlimited power, surrounded by obsequious courtiers who flattered him and catered to every wish and desire, good, bad, indifferent?

Vashti, the queen, deposed because she would not come and show her beauty before a crowd of men who had been on a drunken debauch for a week—Esther 1:10-22. All honour to Vashti, a noble woman!

Mordecai, a Jew, whose people had come from Judah and Jerusalem when Nubuchadnezzar had made them captive—Esther 2:5, 6. He had, evidently, some minor office in the palace. He is a man of strong character and convictions. He is an ardent patriot, looking after the interests of his own people, while loyally serving the Persian ruler—Esther 2:21-23.

Esther around whom the whole action centers. She is a " Maid, fair and beautiful "—Esther 2:7— " Whom Mordecai, when her father and mother were dead, took for his own daughter." She was his cousin.

Haman, a courtier, much thought of by the king. He was advanced, over all the princes to the first place, next to his sovereign—Esther 3:1. He was proud, egotistical and vain and versed in the art of flattery. A small caliber man in a high position. When his vanity was wounded by the refusal of Mordecai to do homage, he showed the cruelty of a ravening wild beast in seeking to destroy the race to which Mordecai belonged.

The Story is of great dramatic power. "Incident after incident is related until the climax of difficulty is reached and the knot is so tied that it seems impossible to escape. Then it is untied with wonderful dexterity."

The Crisis comes after the tales related of the great feasts given by the king and the casting down of Vashti from being queen because of her noble refusal to appear before a drunken crowd of men— chapter one. Esther is made queen in her place— chapter two.

The Interest Begins when Haman, having been advanced to the place next to the king, notices that Mordecai does not bow to him and reverence him—3:1-6. This is such a severe blow to the vanity of Haman that he cannot endure it. He seeks revenge in the most drastic form. He thinks it beneath him to take out his pique on so humble a person as Mordecai. He therefore plots to get a decree from the king to massacre all the Jews, in the kingdom, on a certain day, under the plea that they are a menace to the well-being of the realm—chapter third.

It has been asked—Why did Mordecai refuse to bow to and reverence Haman? It has been replied that Haman, in his extreme vanity, sought to have Divine reverence paid to him, which Mordecai, being

a Jew, could not give him, without renouncing his
religion, which he would not do.

Matters Come to a Head when the king signs the
decree for the destruction of the Jews and a time is
appointed—3:8-15.   Mordecai puts on sackcloth
and ashes and cries aloud in the midst of the city—
4:1-3.   Doubtless Haman is very complacent, rubs
his hands, and smiles and rejoices over the fact that,
at last, he has got his enemy within his grasp.

The Help of Esther is Sought to avert the
awful calamity of the massacre of all the Jews in the
Persian Empire.   The whole matter is set before
Esther, by Mordecai, when she sends to inquire why
he is in sackcloth and ashes.   The demand is made
that she go at once to the king and put the matter up
to him, that a way may be found to set aside the decree of destruction of her people.   The whole action
is found in chapters four to eight.

The First Demand is Made by Mordecai—Esther
4:4-9—when he gives her a copy of the decree.   He
urges her to go before the king immediately.

The Reply of Esther—4:10, 11—is that no one is
allowed to come in unto the king, under pain of
death, unless called.   It is thought that this rule was
made on account of the multitude of backdoor pe-
titions which he had been receiving.   There is a
provision, however, by which, if the king holds out
the golden scepter the petitioner may present a request.   Esther adds, in her reply to Mordecai, that
she has not been called before the king these thirty
days.   She had evidently lost some favour.   This
loss of favour is thought to have been due to the in-
trigue of Haman against her.

The Second Demand of Mordecai is for immediate action. He speaks plainly and bluntly. He
reminds her that she is likely to perish in a general
massacre. Again he tells her that, who knows but
that she has come into her place for just such a
mission—Esther 4:13-17.

The Reply of Esther. She rises to a great act of
renunciation and self-sacrifice. She puts behind her
her love of life and all her ambitions. These must
have been very sweet to her, as a young and beautiful woman, at the beginning of a splendid career.
She sends word to Mordecai, asking him to proclaim
a three days' fast for all the Jews present in Shushan
and that she and her maids will also fast. "And so
will I go in unto the king which is not according to
the law and if I perish, I perish"—Esther 4:16.

**Daring All to Save a People from Extermina-
tion.**—Esther fully realizes the tremendous risk
of her venture. She knows that the favour or dis-
favour of an oriental despot cannot be counted upon
beforehand. So far as possible she will leave nothing
to chance. She has sought Divine approbation by a
fast. She displays good sense in the way she plans
and carries out her plans—chapters five to eight.

Ample Preparation is Made. She puts on her
royal apparel—5:1—making herself as attractive as
possible. Sackcloth and ashes were appropriate for
Mordecai but not for the queen on her present mission. In all this she displayed a remarkable knowledge of human nature, and put it into action.

Waiting a Favourable Opportunity to present her
petition. She might have said—"I have a right
to be heard, I propose to be heard, I will be heard,

because I am the queen." She did nothing of the kind. She did not presume on anything. She stood and waited " In the inner court of the king's house " until the king saw her—5 : 2, 3.

The Right Time Comes. The king sees her and extends to her the golden scepter. There is always a right time but it is not always easy to wait for it as this woman did.

Enlisting the King's Favour that her people may live and not be swept from the surface of the earth. Esther was planning large things and such things need time and care in bringing them to their full fruition. She goes very slowly, feeling her way. Here is no hasty action. Standing there in the court and being asked by the king what her petition is, she realizes that Haman has his friends here, who will report to him at once, any request for the reversal of the decree against the Jews. She exercises a fine sense of wisdom and infinite tact in her reply. She will meet both this Haman and the king together and feel out how matters stand. Here Esther reveals herself as a diplomatic and able woman—chapters 5-7.

The First Banquet. She invites the king and Haman to a feast. She can judge better what to do when Haman is off his guard. But Esther does not get the knowledge she wants at this time. Wise woman! She can wait; hence her invitation to another feast the next night.

In the Interval between the First and Second Banquets, Divine Providence seems to take a hand. Haman cannot wait for the massacre of the Jews to have Mordecai killed and has prepared a gallows to hang him. That night the king cannot sleep and asks that the chronicles of the kingdom be read to him. He finds there that Mordecai has saved his life and that no reward has been given to him— Esther 2: 21-23 and 6: 1-11. Haman is chosen and is obliged, by the king's command, to honour Mordecai by having put on him the king's royal apparel. Then he has to conduct him, on horseback, through the streets proclaiming him as the man whom the king delights to honour. All this is a very bitter thing for Haman, for he had planned this honour for himself.

The Second Banquet. It would seem from the way the narrative reads, that Esther was not yet aware of the honour done for her kinsman. Anyway, at this feast, when the king asks for her petition, she has very evidently made up her mind.

When boldness is required Esther does not hesitate. She at once accuses Haman of the vile plot to destroy her people. She uses in her charge, language that cannot be mistaken. In all this, we have to remember that it is quite a serious thing to accuse a man next to the king in power, of such underhand plotting. " Then Esther the queen answered and said, If I have found favour in thy sight, O king, and if it please the king, let my life be given me at my petition, and my people at my request: For we are sold, I and my people, to be destroyed, to be slain, and to perish. But if we have been sold for bondmen and bondwomen, I had held my tongue, although the enemy could not countervail the king's damage. Then king Ahasuerus answered and said unto Esther, the queen, Who is he and where is he, that durst presume, in his heart to do so? And Esther said, The adversary and enemy is this wicked Haman. Then Haman was afraid before the king and queen "—Esther 7:3-6.

The Character of Esther.—No one can read this book without realizing the strength and power of this woman. She knew how to plan. She knew when to go forward and when to hold back. She could for a great cause calmly risk her life.

Before she was ready to accuse Haman she had gathered all the facts and knew how and when to state her case against him effectually.

Here is no type of a shrinking harem woman, but one who would be an honour to any nation and be a great leader had she lived in our times.

In the End of the Book we find Haman hanged on the gallows he had erected for Mordecai. His place, next to the king, is taken by Mordecai. The king cannot reverse his decree that the Jews be massacred, but he issues new orders that they be allowed to defend themselves from their enemies.

We cannot but wish that the king could have found another way out of his dilemma. We have, however, to remember that "The Oriental Potentate" of a bygone age had very little regard for human life and what he did with it. It was a small matter to him that he sanctioned civil war. We are learning to value human life but we are far from thinking of it as we ought, when we devote such a large portion of our revenues, even in peace times, to forging implements of war. Again, no ancient wars have ever been so destructive as our modern ones.

Questions.—What can be said of Esther as the

heroine of her book? How many chapters in Esther? Where is the scene laid? What can be said of the five principal characters? Describe them. What can be said of this story? What of the crisis—when did it begin, how did matters come to a head? How was the help of Esther sought? Give the two demands of Mordecai and Esther's replies. How did Esther dare all to save her people from destruction, what about the preparation, the favourable opportunity, the right time? How was the king's favour enlisted by the two banquets? What took place in the interval between the banquets? What can be said of the character of Esther? What can be said of the end of the book?

good

XII

WOMAN OF SOLOMON'S SONG

THE SINGLE STANDARD

The Shulamite, of The Song of Solomon, represents a woman faithful to her pledged love amid the seductive temptations of an oriental court.

It is along the same line as the Book of Job where the hero stands true to his convictions when every sort of trial, physical, mental and spiritual, is brought to bear against him.

The Status of Women, in any age, is always an interesting topic. In the time when this poem was written, it was considered quite the proper thing for a king to have a harem in which were sequestered many wives. This was also the rule for his officials. In fact, any man in the kingdom was allowed all the wives he was able to support.

The Watchers for beautiful women for the king's harem were everywhere. These women, married or unmarried, when deemed worthy by their personal charms were brought to the king. If any one pleased the king she became a member of his household. Little or no attention was paid to her former affiliations.

This Country Maiden, in the north, attracted the attention of the king's watchers. She is obliged to come to Jerusalem against her protest. The king is pleased with her, when she is brought before him. He is so much pleased with her that he does not seem to wish to actually force her to enter his harem. On the other hand he seeks to woo her by placing every possible inducement before her of the desirability of court life. It is this wooing, and the refusal of the Shulamite to be won on account of her pledged love to a man, in her home town—one for one—which constitutes the whole action of the book. She does not wish, even with all the inducements the king can offer, to become one of his many wives.

Marriage and Divorce were not under discussion then, as they are to-day, simply because they were so easy to accomplish. When a man got tired of his wife or wives of his youth, he got new ones in one way or another.

All marriages were " Trial Marriages " in which women got the worst of it as they do now in such cases.

The natural result of this practice was the deadening of all the finer feelings of men and women for each other. Men and women degenerated, stepped down, and became beast-like in their loves and hates.

Family life was destroyed. National life decayed. It is no wonder that the kingdom was rent asunder when Solomon died. Of the resultant moral downfall the prophets have much to say. It is all written large in the old records, not only of the Israelites but of the surrounding nations from which they copied the exceedingly loose relations between men and women. It is the same story everywhere with the same results, in those times, of decay and degeneracy of men, women, society and peoples.

It is surprising that to-day, efforts are being so persistently made to turn us back to the old evil practices. The desirability of the marriage relation of one for one, is attacked. Divorce laws are sought to be made easy. Whenever and wherever these things are even partially accomplished the old degeneracy returns, and the human race decays, as of old.

What Solomon's Song is Not.—It is not simply an oriental love song, full of great beauty and charm. On the surface it is exquisite. The movement is light and graceful. The references to pastoral scenes are very frequent. Doves hide in the cleft of the rocks. Gazelles are leaping on the mountains. There are trees with varied foliage and flowers with bright hues and rich perfume. We seem to walk in vineyards and amidst fig trees, in the balmy air of spring. But if this book was only and solely a beautiful poem it would never have found a place in the canon of Scripture.

What the Woman, in the Song, Stands For.— No one can read this poem without feeling the deep undercurrent of feeling that only flows in one direction. What is that direction? What does the Shulamite want?

She is in Favour of "The Pair Marriage." She wants to be returned to her northern home and to her affianced husband. This is the burden of her every utterance. No matter how much below the king he is, she can love no one else. All the riches and all the greatness of the gorgeous court life cannot win her away, however beautifully they may be displayed.

She does not want to share her love with another man any more than she wants her affianced husband to share his love with another woman.

Here is a Protest against polygamy, written at a time when this was the almost universal practice. We begin to see now why this song has a place in the Bible. This protest speaks for all time against anything but "The Pair Marriage." Hence, here we have no reference to "The Mosaic Law" or the peculiar institutions of Judaism.

Here are shining the purity and constancy of a woman's love. Here is an example, an ideal, for all time, of the religion of true love between a man and a woman, which makes possible the flourishing of the virtues of a worth-while family life and the building up of a people into a truly great nation.

Here is a Voice in the midst of a corrupt age, lifted up for purity of life and a return to the right relations, ordained of God, between men and women. It is against the lower ideals of free love and loose practices, in marriage and divorce, which ought to be forever cast out from human society.

There Are Three Attempts of the King to Win the Shulamite, for his harem, and away from the man to whom she is betrothed. They are plainly set forth in the poem. They have been classified as follows:

First Attempt. After the introduction—1:1—the court ladies engage the Shulamite—1:2-8. A chorus of virgins praise the king—1:2-4. The Shulamite expresses her opinion of herself and her longing for her Northern home—1:5-7. The chorus answers—1:8.

Solomon now enters as a suitor. He says—1:9-17 —"I have compared thee, O my love, to a company of horses in Pharaoh's chariots. Thy cheeks are comely with rows of jewels, thy neck with chains of gold. We will make thee borders of gold studded with silver." . . . "Behold thou art fair, my love, behold thou art fair; thou hast doves' eyes," etc.

First Repulse. But the mind of the maiden is far away. She seems not to pay heed to the king's flatteries. She has no use for him. She hears another voice calling her, that of her affianced husband. She says—2:8-10—"The voice of my beloved! Behold he cometh, leaping upon the mountains and skipping on the hills." . . . "My beloved spake and said unto me, Rise up, my love, my fair one, and come away." *Read the whole second chapter* in this connection. In the latter part of this chapter she seems to recall scenes from her past life when she was happy in her northern home.

In chapter 3:1-5, she has a dream in which she seems to go in search of the beloved one of her Northern home.

Second Attempt. Solomon is seen approaching in royal state. His greatness and glory are shown the Shulamite—3:6-11. He praises her beauty in the most exquisite terms of endearment—4:1-7.

Second Repulse. The flatteries of the king bring no response. The Shulamite's thoughts are far away, as they were before. She is not at all impressed by the greatness and glory of the king. His riches are as nothing to her compared to her faithful love. After all, she knows that the king has probably uttered these flatteries many times before under the same circumstances, and that she, if she yields, will only be a passing fancy. Shortly she will be compelled to give place to a newer beautiful face which is the case with all free lovers and loose observers of marriage vows. It may be also that she has some friend in the north, who has been invited in by the front door of the harem, and cast out at the back as

"Useless Baggage." In her reply The Shulamite expresses her longing for and belief in her "Beloved One"—4:8-5:1. Again she dreams that she seeks him in vain throughout the city—5:2-8.

Third Attempt. The ladies of the king's court, or harem, now again take a hand in the matter.

They say in substance, "Why should you set yourself above your fellows?" "Why go beyond the standards of your time?" "Why be prudish?" "Do as others do." "Do you not know that many women consider it an honour to be invited into the king's harem?" Here is what they say, in the exact words of the text—"What is thy beloved more than another beloved, O thou fairest among women? What is thy beloved more than another beloved, that thou dost so charge us?"—5:9. It is the same sort of argument that we hear to-day from the advocates of what they call "Free Marriage and Divorce." The Shulamite's answer of faithful love is given in chapter 5:10-6:3. She would impress upon the ladies of the court her love and faithfulness to one and not to many.

Solomon seconds the effort of his harem women in renewed flatteries—"Thou art beautiful, O my love, as Tirzah, comely as Jerusalem, terrible as an army with banners. Turn away thine eyes from me for they have overcome me," etc.—6:4-7:9.

It is the same old story to-day, of the man of many loves to win a new one. But what can this king offer The Shulamite? He confesses to having "Threescore queens and fourscore concubines and virgins without number"—6:8. His is a jaded and worn-out love stimulated, it may be now, by this woman's pretty face and her refusal to enter his harem.

The Third Repulse. This is the final one. This maiden, of the long ago, shows she has read this age-old " Man of the World " who is still with us setting his snares to catch the unwary ones.

The Triumph of the Shulamite is complete —7 : 10-8 : 14. Note her confidence. She says—" I am my beloved's and his desire is towards me." " Come, my beloved, let us go forth into the field ; let us lodge in the villages "—7 : 10-11. To be with the " One " she loves in the fields and villages, in the humble walks of life, is more than to be lodged in the palace of the king, one amongst many or one in a procession.

A Final Strong Tribute to a Faithful Love is given in chapter 8 : 6, 7. " Set me a seal upon thine heart, as a seal upon thine arm : for love is strong as death : jealousy as cruel as the grave : the coals thereof are coals of fire which hath a most vehement flame. Many waters cannot quench love, neither can floods drown it : if a man would give all the substance of his house for love, it would utterly be contemned."

Questions.—What does the Shulamite represent ? What can be said of the status of women ? What can be said of the watchers for women ? What can be said of the country maiden from the north ? What can be said of marriage and divorce in the olden days ? What Solomon's Song is not. What does the woman, in the song, stand for ? What about the favour, the protest, the voice ? Give an account of the three attempts of the king to win the Shulamite and his three repulses. What of the triumph of the Shulamite ?

XIII

MOTHER OF JESUS

BEST AND BEST KNOWN

Mary, The Mother of Jesus, is better known than any other woman in the Bible. She is the best known woman in the world of to-day. She is in the white light of a pitiless and persistent publicity. Her every act, word and attitude, has been and is most carefully scrutinized. It was said to her—" Blessed art thou among women "—Luke 1 : 28. After many centuries have passed that statement still stands unquestioned.

She Had No Easy Life. At first the glorious prophecies concerning the career of her son raised her expectations to the highest point. These must have been dimmed in the long monotonous years of waiting, in the home life in Nazareth, when her son became a village carpenter. What disappointment, even if unrecorded, must have been hers!

After thirty years of waiting, her Son became the most famous man in all Palestine. Multitudes followed Him everywhere. He charmed people by His gracious words. He did many marvelous things. He was proclaimed as " The Son of God " and " The Son of Man." But the sky of His splendid career darkens. He is arrested and tried for His life. He is condemned to be crucified. His mother's heart is torn asunder with horror and grief. How can she survive this awful calamity?

The sky brightens. " The Resurrection Day " dawns, her Son rises from the dead, and she ascends to the heights of joy. For some of the Scripture references read—Matthew 1:18-2:23; Luke first and second chapters; John second chapter; Matthew 12:46-50; John 19:25-27; Acts 1:14.

How Judged?—By what standard, or standards, can we make a true estimate of the life, conduct, and character of Mary?

Some Common Methods of Judging Women are by—

Beauty of face and form. Hence the efforts made to be attractive.

Dress. Hence the great desire for outward adornment.

Occupation. Hence the rush for the better places.

Social position and wealth. Hence the eagerness to excell.

Cleverness. The woman with brains goes far. Hence the multitude of colleges.

Character, the salt, without which the others lose their flavor.

We get many and varied results in judging by the above, singly or in combinations.

Still other Ways must be sought, to get at the excellencies of Mary. Nothing is said of her beauty in the Scriptures, although the most eminent artists have vied with each other in painting what they imagined the beauty of her face to be like, in their " Madonnas." We find no word set down about her outward adornment. We know that she was poor and had no high social standing. No one doubts her strong character.

She was, according to the record, a humble village woman, living in a small town. This little place was so insignificant as to lead a great man to say—" Can any good thing come out of Nazareth? "—John 1: 46. Yet, in the Bible and outside, she has been given the highest place among women.

She Excelled in the Qualities which are most needed everywhere. When adopted, and practised, they exalt and make glorious any woman, in any walk of life. They are not dependent upon, but independent of, and go with or without beauty, dress, social rank, wealth and cleverness. We consider some of these qualities, which like the rays of the sun, gild all those upon whom they shine, with a golden light.

The Quality of Her Pre-Eminent Faith, which comprehended what was being said to her and took it at its true value. She was not credulous. She asked intelligent questions of the angel as to what he meant by the statement that she would be the " Mother of Jesus "—Luke 1: 28-45. Here is a highly intelligent mind seeking to know the exact status of things. When convinced of the genuineness of the message, she accepted, with great faith, all that the angel implied in it. Some of the things the angel set forth are yet to be fulfilled, such as—" Of His kingdom there shall be no end "—Luke 1: 33.

It was a tremendous feat of her faith, as we look back upon it now, and see all that has come to pass, to see things as Gabriel saw them and wanted Mary to see them. In the like manner we are called upon to have faith that God can and will take care of the future, our future as well as the future of the world. Life is really worth the living when this sort of faith is attained. Without it, life is cast into—"The shallows and quicksands."

The Quality of Her Joy and Gladness.—In Mary we find no grim determination to do and dare for her faith. It is on a higher level. She does what she does because she is wonderfully pleased to do it. Listen to what she says in her song of rejoicing, in "The Magnificat": "My soul doth magnify the Lord and my spirit hath rejoiced in God, my Saviour. For he hath regarded the low estate of his handmaiden: for behold from henceforth all generations shall call me blessed. For he that is mighty hath done to me great things; and holy is his name. . . . He hath put down the mighty from their seats and exalted them of low degree, etc."—Luke 1:46-55. She shows here poetic and prophetic genius of the highest order. Notice the "all generations shall call me blessed;" not alone Jew, Roman, Greek, but "All." Thus, at the very beginning, she foretells the world-wide scope of the message of "The Christ."

Suppose, just suppose, that every child should be given the glad welcome into this world that Mary gave to Jesus! It is to the rejoicing element and quality, that we desire to call attention. It gives wings to her faith which lift her above being perplexed by the sordid things of earth. It is the quality that is needed in our faith to-day.

The Quality of Her Far-Seeing Vision.—She had the long look into the future. She saw things not as they are, confused and jumbled and hard to understand, but as they are to be. Often things must seem to be jumbled and confused before the more perfect order comes to pass. The contractor, in building a great, tall, many storied structure, must often first tear down a number of smaller buildings and blast out a deep rock foundation. To one looking on, the tearing down and blasting out processes seem only destructive; but every step to the builder, who has the plan in mind, is one of construction. He sees what is to be, not what is. Mary saw the plan for the bettering of the world. She saw her part in it, as every woman has a part, and was satisfied to work to that end.

Every life coming into this world is a new possibility for good or evil. We know this by seeing what the lives that have come and gone have accomplished. No place so small, no city so large, but what this is being continually demonstrated. Mary, looking far into the future, by what she has been told, will be the instrument used to set up a life whose influence for good will never be exhausted. There is nothing so heartening as this " Vision of the Future."

The Quality of Keeping Her Ideals Unsullied and holding steadily on her way. There are many things that would tend to dim the ideals of Mary. Keeping house with the scanty means and few conveniences that she had was not very nourishing to great thoughts. Doing the same things, day after day, and with no change, as the dreary years went by would naturally sully the best ideals.

Monotony is the worst foe of the higher things of life. Then too, contact, daily contact, with any one, however great, is apt to be disillusioning, not because there is not true greatness to be considered but because of our own lowering of our estimations.

But wherever and whenever the curtain lifts and we get a view of Mary she has the very same spirit that she had when she composed her song of rejoicing—" The Magnificat."

The Quality of Conquering Her Perplexities and Anxieties.—They must have been many considering what she had been called upon to believe. Jesus, as a baby, must have had the usual sicknesses. As a boy he must have had the usual boy troubles. As a young man, going out as a carpenter, day after day, to help build houses or do odd jobs, she must have been often asking herself the question—" Is this really the Messiah?" "Can this be ' The One ' who is to bless the whole world, ' The One ' whom I see at the table every day and who goes to his work every morning?"

If she had perplexities, she kept them to herself, so far as we know. She was not of that number who continually bombard you with their troubles and make life a burden. Mary must have been a fine hostess when people came visiting, for she seems to have had so many cheering things to say.

The Quality of Her Humility.—Mary seems mindful that she is a humble village maiden. She says—" For he hath regarded the low estate of his handmaiden "—Luke 1:48. She never seems to claim anything for herself. It is all for her Son. It is one of the remarkable, and also one of the sad things in the history of Christendom, that she has been selected as one of the objects of worship by a certain church and that prayers should be offered up to her and incense waved before her. She would be one of the first to repudiate this sort of thing could she come to earth again. Nowhere in the New Testament can be found any such claim for Mary by herself or others for her. Everywhere that she is mentioned, in any way, we see her humility.

The Quality of Her Reverence.—Her worship is for her Son. At the very beginning she said— " My soul doth magnify the Lord. And my spirit hath rejoiced in God, my Saviour "—Luke 1:46, 47. In this belief she never seems to have wavered. It is something to be said, and it cannot be too strongly emphasized, that " The Manhood of the Master " never shone forth more clearly than it did in the narrow and confined quarters of that small house in Nazareth.

The Quality of Her Faithfulness at the Cross.—The last few days of Christ's life on earth must have been heartbreaking ones for his mother. She had come down from her home town expecting? Who knows what she expected? She remembered what high hopes she had when he was born, what the angel had said to her, the visit of " The Wise Men " and of " The Shepherds." Now would her Son reveal himself for what He was? Would He be proclaimed as The Messiah?

When on Palm Sunday she heard the multitudes shouting " Hosannas " in His name and looking to Him as the " One " who was to redeem Israel, what would come to pass? Everything seemed possible. All her visions seemed to be coming true.

But the scene rapidly changes. He is arrested. He is taken for trial before the hostile high priests. He is condemned by Pilate. He must suffer death on the cross. Everything that has been worth while is broken and shattered. The earthquake has come. It is the end. Behold, the unhappy mother! But if she is unhappy no one knows it. All honour to her. She has not lost her faith and is faithful. The curtain lifts and we see Mary at the cross, close to it, that her Son may see her. She will give Him all the aid and comfort that she can. Her Son sees her and commends her to John, who takes her to his own home—John 19:25-27.

The Last View of Christ's Mother (Acts 1 : 12-14—is at the first meeting of a few of the disciples after the resurrection and ascension. All is changed. Everything is cleared up. Jesus has come to life again. The new hope is borne in upon the world. The believing faithful mother is right at the beginning of things, in the new beginning, as she was at the first. Everything that the angel Gabriel told Mary, at first, has been fulfilled, except the things of the far-future.

She is the First Among Women.—In the Bible there is no name which stands before hers. In Christian lands her name is the first. Outside Christian countries she is known, wherever Jesus Christ is known, as the " Mother of Our Lord," the best known of all mothers.

Why Does She Take Such a High Position?—Because of her mother-relation to Jesus Christ? Yes, and more, because she gave herself up to be possessed of a great faith and high ideals. She placed her life in their keeping and they have carried her far, through her Saviour and Son, in whom she trusted implicitly.

Questions.—What can be said of Mary, the

mother of Jesus? Did she have an easy life? How
judged? What are common methods of judging
women? What ways ought to be applied to Mary?
How and why is she the best and best known woman?
What can be said of her pre-eminent faith; her joy
and gladness; her far-seeing vision? How did she
keep her ideals unsullied and how did she conquer
her perplexities? What can be said of her humility;
her reverence for her Son? What can be said of her
faithfulness at the cross? What is the last view of
Christ's mother? Why is she first among women?
Why does she take such a high position?

miracl at Cana — whatever he say do it — just like a mother

XIV

WIFE OF PETER

A HIDDEN WOMAN

Did Peter Have a Wife?—The common supposition is that he did not. But this supposition is contrary to fact. In proof that he did have a wife, we turn to two passages of Scripture—

First—Matthew 8:14. We here find an account of Jesus coming to the city of Capernaum—Matthew 8:1-15—and while there he came to Peter's house—"And when Jesus was come into Peter's house, he saw his wife's mother laid and sick of a fever and he touched her hand and the fever left her." If Peter had a mother-in-law he must have had a wife.

Second—I Corinthians 9:5. It is quite evident that his wife accompanied him when he went on his missionary journeys. She might have helped him in many ways, personally, and in seeing the carefully secluded women of the east and giving them the Gospel message. Speaking of this practice, of the wives of the early missionaries going with them, Paul says—"Have we not power to lead about a sister, a wife, as well as other apostles, and as the brethren of the Lord and Cephas (Peter)?"

Why is Not More Said About Peter's Wife?—That we do not know. The same question might be asked about the wives of many men who figure prominently, inside and outside the Bible. We know that they had homes and families but no details are given.

A Hidden Woman.—Peter's wife belonged in the class of what are known as " The Hidden Women." Their number is very large. It was very much larger in the time when the New Testament was written than it is to-day. They are not hidden in the sense that they are shut up somewhere or concealed so that people may not see them or that they are, in any way, deprived of their liberty. They may be very much in evidence and yet be hidden in the sense that they are practically unknown beyond their own households and a very limited circle of friends and acquaintances. These women may be very gifted, in many ways, have fine personalities, and exceedingly efficient, but with no opportunity to express themselves. They are " The Real Shut Ins."

Hidden Behind a Husband's Reputation.— Peter's work bulks large in the New Testament. He is one of the most prominent figures. He is the chief of the Apostles in The Gospels. He takes first place in The Acts for the first twelve chapters.

His place is not usurped. He comes rightly by it. He is energetic, enthusiastic, full of faith in his Master, Jesus Christ, and willing to do and to dare for Him. Although married, he is looked upon as the first pope, but that there was any pope at that time is denied. He was very prominent in the affairs of the early Christian churches.

What chance was there for his wife to be known under the shadow of such a great reputation? Not very much. Still if we speculate a little. She certainly must have been a discreet woman, for she did nothing to injure his fame. She might have done very much in helping him gain and hold what he had. We know that naturally Peter was an impulsive man and who knows how often Peter might have come home, ready to give things up, and had his wife caution him to go slowly and think before he acted as many a good wife has done with that kind of a husband.

In his missionary tours she must have been of no small assistance, for otherwise he could not have taken her. There were at that time no great Foreign Missionary Societies, with funds, to send out labourers into needy fields and everyone who went on tours of this sort had to look out for himself.

Hidden Behind Household Cares.—The keeping of a house in order and the getting of meals regularly, and on time, are no easy matters. They, by their regularity and monotony, often become very irksome. It is a round and round sort of business which cannot be shirked for the welfare of the members of the home depend upon its being well done.

Sickness lays extra burdens upon willing hands. In all probability Peter's wife had her hands full with her household duties and when her mother was taken sick with a fever, while eager to do all she could, she might have been much overburdened.

Therefore when Jesus Christ unexpectedly came to her home and healed her mother, she was very grateful and very much relieved. Her mother, when cured of her fever, arose and helped with the getting the house in order again; for in sickness, much housework has to be neglected and only the necessary things done.

Peter's wife would, doubtless, have been very glad to have gone out of the house with her husband, down by the seaside, and to have listened to what "The Wonderful Christ" was saying and to have seen Him open the eyes of the blind, cause the lame to walk, and heal all manner of diseases. But she must attend to her household and be hidden behind its duties so that when its members came home all things might be in readiness for them.

All honour to the women, standing like Peter's wife by their homes, subordinating their desires and their pleasures to keeping things up, where they need to be kept up, and doing an exceedingly important work.

Hidden Behind the Children of the Home.—We find no mention or hint of any children in the Capernaum household. While there might have been children, we have no right to speculate. But where there are children, in the home, it is the wife and mother who has to bear the chief burden of their daily care and upbringing.

She it is who subordinates herself to them. Often, too often, she not only is hidden behind what they want to do, and propose to do, but forgotten. Burdens are placed upon her shoulders which she is ill able to bear. If it is a question of going without, it is not the children, but mother. It is mother who bears the heat and burden of the day when the children go to school. She must be behind the meals to get them strictly on time. When it is college, for the boy or girl, it is mother who gives up this and that, in order that the coveted diploma may be had.

It is time that we brought mother out and let her have some of the good times to which she is entitled.

There are extravagant, lazy, gay, good-for-nothing types of women, as there are of men. We are not

writing of them in this connection. We are only saying some words, which cannot be said too often, for
the women who subordinate themselves to their
households and get no recognition for it.

**Women Hidden Behind the Modern Business
Men.**—Now we leave the first century and come
to the twentieth. Is everything changed and different? We try to make ourselves believe that it is. But
we find here, as late as it is, that " The Hidden
Woman " is still with us—behind her husband's reputation, household cares and children.

Now we have a new class to deal with in addition
to wives and mothers. It is the class of young women
secretaries, teachers, stenographers, clerks and others,
who are out in the modern business world and who
are taking upon themselves its cares and putting themselves under its burdens.

Just here new forces are at work and new intel-
ligencies are solving age old problems. Work is being arranged so that all of it cannot be piled upon one
willing pair of shoulders in any certain work.
Churches, women's societies and clubs are agitating
on every hand, a new order of things in the woman's
world, in giving woman a fair chance.

The Conclusion of the Whole Matter.—That
is the old matter like the closing up one volume to
open another. The agitation for a fair deal for
women was begun in the teaching of the New Testament. It has been in agitation ever since.

The ideal of the Greek and the Roman was the
slave one for women; the plaything and the chattel
of man. She must bear, uncomplainingly, all the
burdens placed upon her. It has been hard to kill

that ideal. Notice how Peter, himself, advancing, writes of this question in his First Epistle 3:1-12. He begins with the old idea.

First, of subjection of the wife to the husband, 3:1.

Second, of giving honour unto the wife, as the weaker vessel, 3:7.

Third, of the equality of the wife with the husband, " Finally, be ye all of one mind, having compassion one for another . . . not rendering evil for evil, or railing for railing: but contrariwise blessing: knowing that ye are thereunto called, that ye should inherit a blessing—3:8, 9. Or we can go back beyond the New Testament to the Old Testament where, in Genesis 2:18, 23, 24, woman is shown as man's equal, companion and helpmeet.

The Last Word in a Right Way of Looking at Things.—When we come to understand and exalt the Biblical teachings of the proper relations of husband to wife and of men and women, in general, to each other we may find it our glory to put ourselves under burdens and to be hidden in our work that that work may be exalted, even as Jesus Christ humbled himself to carry the burden of the world. It is certainly a fact that the person who continually puts himself or herself forward and calls attention to what is being done becomes, in time, rather of a nuisance.

It is one thing to have a burden thrust upon us, that we do not want. It is quite another thing to take up and carry a burden, even if it is twice as heavy, but which is self-imposed. Many a woman, and many a man, is willing to be put in an obscure place and loaded down with work if it is felt that thereby good is being accomplished.

It may be that the wife of Peter wanted to be hidden in order that the great cause in which she believed might be advanced.

Questions.—Did Peter have a wife? Give the Scripture proofs. Why is not more said about Peter's wife? What can be said about Peter's wife as a hidden woman? What can be said of being hidden behind a husband's reputation; household cares; the children in the home; the modern business man? What is the conclusion of the whole matter? What is the last word in a right way of looking at things?

XV

A WOMAN OF SAMARIA

A KEEN QUESTIONER

The Questioner?—A Woman of Samaria (John 4:4-42), who talked with Jesus, near her home town, by a well where she had gone to draw water.

Her wits had been sharpened by some bitter experiences with an unfriendly world. Her tongue was facile in asking about things which she knew perfectly well would provoke controversy. She seemed to delight in touching sore spots with no gentle hand. As she had been badly treated by life, she would take it out on others. None too good; her matrimonial experiences, with five husbands, had evidently soured a naturally cheerful disposition.

But with all her handicaps, her mind seemingly unaffected, brooded over the great questions of God, life and destiny, although she sullenly revolted at the bad conditions in which she found herself.

When, therefore, she saw a stranger, Jesus, by the well, she was all ready to begin a wordy battle and to match her wits against His.

The signal to start the verbal contest was given when Jesus asks for a drink of water. Instead of giving it to Him, seeing that he is a Jew, she says— " How is it that thou, being a Jew, askest drink of me which am a woman of Samaria? For the Jews have no dealings with the Samaritans." This is the first one about race, of the four great controversial questions which she raises.

The Answerer, Jesus Christ, is entirely different from any one whom she has encountered. He is not provoked into bitter retorts to which she has become accustomed. He replies, directly and indirectly, to her attacking questions, in such a way, that she is astounded. No one has answered her in like fashion. Here are real replies to questions which she had thought unanswerable. She is so satisfied that she has not the heart to continue. She is told that much of her trouble comes from the tumult and unrest in her own heart.

Finally she is so amazed by the wonder of it all that she forgets what she has come to the well for and starts back to her little city without her water pot. There she goes up and down the streets urging the people to come and see the wonderful man who has told her so much and so well. A marvelous change of front for this worldly wise cynical woman!

The Four Great Questions, brought up by the Samaritan woman, are still with us, in one form or another. They deal with the very foundations of things. They have not been settled because the world has not yet been brought to the " Christ Basis " of settlement. We are still in the " Woman of Samaria Stage of Things," questioning for the sake of questioning, with no real desire to apply the right remedies, even when known. Let us consider these questions separately:

1—What Keeps Races Apart?—" The Jews have no dealings with the Samaritans," declared the Samaritan Woman. Why not? Physically they are made the same. They require the same food. They labour at the same tasks. They have like hopes and ambitions. They have the same sort of mental outfits. They have a like length of years. They suffer from the same diseases. They thrive alike under good governments and go down under bad. What was true of the Jews and Samaritans in the olden time is true of races and peoples to-day.

There is no law which sets apart certain sections of our big and little cities for Russians, Poles, Italians, Jews, and other nationalities. The races segregate themselves. They do not wish to mingle. This is one of the great arguments for those, at the present day, who oppose unrestricted immigration into our country in that the people, who come, propose to retain their own national customs and habits.

What is the Real Trouble? First, the accentuation of race differences. America for Americans. England for Englishmen. France for Frenchmen and so on. The Jews and Samaritans cultivated and made much of their own customs and manners and worship.

Second, the keeping, at the front, race dislike, prejudice and hatred; especially the hatred. It is the latter which principally kept Jews and Samaritans apart. It is this that still keeps races apart. It splits up families. It spoils friendships. It causes wars to begin and go on to bitter and disastrous ends. When race hatred ceases, no war will be possible.

The Solution and Answer which Christ Proposed, to the Woman of Samaria, still stands as the way out of the difficulty. " If thou knewest the gift of God and who it is that saith to thee, Give me to drink, thou wouldst have asked of him, and he would have given thee living water." He is referring here to his words of peace and good will which, if accepted, would bring to an end the hatreds, jealousies and prejudices of nations, races and peoples.

Christ was ever talking, not about a " New Kingdom of The Jews " triumphant over all, but a " Kingdom of God, of Righteousness, and Peace." It was not a restricted but a universal one. He is the first advocate of " The World State."

2—Where is the Proper Place of Worship?— Man has been called a " Religious Animal." Wipe out religion to-day and it will be back to-morrow. Man ever seeks a place to express himself in devotional acts. Where is the proper place? The Jews had a place. The Samaritans had a place. Which was the right one? The Samaritan Woman said— " Our fathers worshipped in this mountain; and ye say that in Jerusalem is the place where men ought to worship." This had been the subject of long-drawn out controversies. The religions of the world are even now divided on this subject of proper places of worship, and the forms to be observed. Which is right? has been, is now, the cause of bitter feelings.

Here is a fine chance for debate. Shrewd kings and rulers of men, knowing the force of the religious motive, have ever accentuated the desirability of a purely national religion and places of worship. The old kings of Israel understood this when the division came, after the rule of King Solomon. In our cities and towns it still causes divisions and dissensions, as to which is the right creed to believe and ritual to be observed.

The Way Out of this Difficulty was plainly shown by Jesus Christ. He did not enter into the controversy as to which was the right temple of worship.

Notice His reply—"Woman, believe me, the hour cometh, when ye shall neither in this mountain, nor yet at Jerusalem, worship the Father . . . But the hour cometh, and now is, when the true worshippers shall worship the Father in spirit and in truth: for the Father seeketh such to worship him." Places and times and forms of worship will be no longer in controversy when this simple Christ solution of the matter is accepted. Anywhere, and at any time, man can turn to the worship of the Father.

3—**Who is the Right Object of Worship?**—It would seem as if some question of the Samaritan Woman had been dropped out, between verses 23 and 24 and that it had something to do with, "Who would be worshipped?" With the idolatrous worship that was all around and the numerous idols such a question would have been perfectly in order.

The importance of this question of "Who is God?" and his relation to man, cannot be overestimated. For according to the answers given, men have loved or hated each other. They have lived good, true, upright, honest lives or they have steeped themselves in evil and, indulging in every bad passion, they have become like beasts of the field. They have built up or torn down society and the state. They have cultivated every grace and lived in brotherly love or they have exalted hatred and offered human sacrifices. The difference between races and nations is not so much in climate, land, government, as it is in the ideal of the religion which is professed.

The Greatness of the Reply of Jesus to the implied question as to "Who is God?" and "Who is the right object of worship?" has never been surpassed,

"God is a spirit and they that worship him must worship him in spirit and in truth." He is a Personal Spirit. He is in His universe and over it, and greater than it; seeing all, ruling all, caring for all. He loves and cares for each and every individual. Jesus said, in the previous chapter, to Nicodemus,— John 3:16—"For God so loved the world that he gave his only begotten Son, that whosoever believeth in him should not perish, but have everlasting life. For God sent not his Son into the world to condemn the world; but that the world through him might be saved."

4—Who is the Messiah and When Will He Come?—The Samaritans and Jews, both, expected the Messiah. Three important questions have been asked and fairly and adequately answered. That which was begun in the spirit of controversy, by the Woman of Samaria, has resulted in the most enlightening religious discussion ever held.

All the principles by which nations can be brought together, and peoples and races made happy, have been set forth. Now remains the question of personal leadership with both the Jew and Samaritan conceded to the Messiah.

This was the fourth question of the Samaritan Woman, that about the coming of The Messiah. "The woman saith unto him, I know that Messias cometh, which is called Christ: when he is come, he will tell us all things." What must have been the astonishment of the woman when—*Jesus Answered* "I that speak unto thee am he." Here is a direct declaration of what Christ is by Himself. What could be more clear and plain than this?

The Questions are Ended.—Action begins.

The spirit of the woman is changed. Her whole outlook on life is different. You can feel, in reading the narrative, that someway and somehow, her gloom and depression have departed. The old cynical attitude is gone. She is alive and active with new and great purposes. She is so filled with enthusiasm for The Messiah, whom she has found, that she wants to tell every one. She starts, at once, back home, forgetting her water pot, to tell all her neighbours.

Her neighbours, seeing the changes wrought in this woman, flock out to see The Christ. They are convinced as the woman was. They invite Him to be their guest, which He is for two days. Many put their faith in him.

When Christ departs from the city, the people tell the Samaritan Woman—" Now we believe not because of thy saying: for we have heard him ourselves, and know that this is indeed the Christ, the Saviour of the world."

Questions.—What can be said of the questioner, the woman of Samaria? What can be said of the answerer, Jesus Christ; how did He reply? What can be said of the four great questions brought up by the woman? 1—What keeps races apart; what is the reply of Jesus? 2—Where is the proper place of worship; what is the way out of this difficulty? 3—Who is the right object of worship? What can be said about the greatness of the reply of Jesus? 4—Who is the Messiah and when will he come? What was the reply of Jesus? What can be said about the ending of the questions? What about the change wrought in the woman of Samaria? What did the people of the city do and say about the Christ?

XVI

MARTHA AND MARY

A TASK AND A VISION

In Martha's House.—The incident related, in Luke 10: 38-42, in the life of the famous New Testament sisters, took place, in their home, in the village of Bethany.

It is stated that the house belonged to Martha. Houses differ as much as the people who dwell in them. Some are well kept and some are not. But we may rest assured that, in this one everything was in good order all the time. Nothing was out of place.

The owner was a painfully neat woman who prided herself on her good housekeeping. All the people in the village knew her for her excellent qualities, but they did not go to her house unless they were dressed in accordance with its neatness. Martha worked hard to maintain her standard and she wanted everyone else to conform to it.

A Hostess' Treatment of Her Guest.—The situation is an interesting one.

Martha is the one who invites Jesus into her home. Mary comes into the story later on. There is no question of faith involved. The sisters believe in Christ. There is no doubt but that The Master loved to be entertained in this neat and orderly home where there was always a warm welcome and good fare. Who would not? The point at issue is not the good way of keeping house. Doubtless this would have

120

been praised, as it deserved to be, had the subject come up, but it did not. Women like Martha are worthy of all commendation.

The matter to be considered is that the hostess forgot herself in the ill treatment of an invited guest. What Martha says about her cares and being left alone to serve would be enough to make anyone feel that his presence was unwelcome.

The Conditions of Oppression, under which Martha felt herself to be, were that she " Was cumbered with much serving." The receiving of a guest put her out of her daily routine and caused things to become, to her mind, somewhat disorderly. This irked her and she became irritable. We can seem to hear the querulous manner in which she speaks.

A Direct Complaint is made to her guest of the burden that His entertainment involves. " Lord, dost thou not care that my sister hath left me to serve alone?" It is as though she had said—"You see, do you not, how I am striving to entertain you, and doing all the work, while you sit there and talk with my sister." It does not seem to occur to Martha that Mary might have been trying to make Jesus welcome also. But this remark of Martha's seems almost as much aimed at Jesus as at her sister. It certainly was a rather embarrassing situation to say the least.

A Request for Interference in a Family Affair. It is always a delicate and hazardous thing, even if asked, to step between relatives in a matter at which they are at odds. To do so, even with the best of intentions, to settle the matter in dispute, is often to acquire the enmity of both parties. Martha ought not to have asked her guest to correct her sister, as she did in saying, " Bid her therefore that she help me."

The Rebuke of Jesus. We marvel at His self-restraint. Many a guest would have felt that he had been badly treated at hearing Martha's outburst. He might have said hard things in reply, or He might have left the house in indignation. But Jesus takes an entirely different way, an unexpected way. He recognizes Martha's overcare for His welfare and how, through this very anxiety, she has grown irritable. He sees the excellent qualities of this good woman behind her complaints.

It is a gentle rebuke that He administers, when he says—" Martha, Martha, thou art careful and troubled about many things." His very tones of voice must have soothed her irritability. He knew Martha and He was not too warped in His judgment by what she said under the stress of strong feelings.

The Attitude of Mary. She heard what her sister said about her and of what she accused her. She might have had much to say in her own defense. We would certainly have liked to hear her side of the case. She might have caused us to take an entirely different view from what is now taken. But she met the accusations of her sister in silence. She would not quarrel about the matter. Why should she? Nothing is to be gained by hurling back counter accusations, when unjustly, or what seems unjustly, attacked.

It may have been this " Attitude of Mary " which led Jesus to say—" But one thing is needful: and Mary hath chosen that good part which shall not be taken away from her."

A Reason for Martha's Action.—In the New

Testament narratives meaning often lies below meaning. Truth underlies truth.

According to a popular view of this story, Martha was the practical woman, and Mary the visionary one. Martha was up and doing and wanted to see things go. She seems to have been impatient with anything that did not get at immediate results.

Mary, on the other hand, was contemplative. She was visionary. " She sat at Jesus' feet and heard his word."

Martha, evidently, never wanted to see perfectly good hours wasted, as she might have called it, in just thinking and talking over matters. If anyone was not actively engaged in doing something with her hands, or going on some good errand, she was looked upon as an idler.

Seeing Life as a Task—The Martha Way.— Walking, in this way, is a large class of women. Life is a hardship. Life is a drudgery. There is no good thing in it. It is work, work, work, day after day. The burden of it is felt to press down very hard and, as the days go by, to get still harder. This road of " A Task " is full of complainers, as it is a difficult road to travel. There are few, if any, pleasant views. It is a peculiarity that although it is a crowded way, every one traveling on it seems to walk it alone. There are places so hazardous that they seem impossible to be passed and women have been known to throw themselves down to the rocks below, rather than to attempt passage. Travelers, on this way, are of all classes, rich, poor, wise, ignorant, well and poorly dressed. There are those who are conscientious in doing what they are called upon to do, as they go along and doing it well, but who see no light of hope at the end. There are also the soured and the bitter ones.

It has been suggested, considering all aspects of this question, that this—" Seeing Life as a Hard Road to Travel "— may be in our attitude of mind toward it, rather than in the road itself. Life has tasks and hard ones. It is not, however, that life is so difficult in itself, as it is in the manner in which it is considered. A light burden, for which one can see no reason at all, becomes a very heavy one; while a very heavy burden becomes a light one when it is assumed because it is wanted and in a good cause. So far as can be judged, by the narrative, Martha had little occasion to act as she did. Life taken purely as " A Task " is the hardest kind of drudgery.

Seeing Life as a Vision—The Mary Way.— Here again there is the danger of one-sidedness. Life is seen as an illusion that is not worth taking seriously. There is no thought of attempting to take up any burden so that the task of life is not felt. Here is where some would place Mary and would accuse her of only thinking of a visionary contemplation of Jesus and His mission. Women in this class of " Pure Visionaries " never regard anything seriously. They do not take to heart household or any other duties. They will accept any appointment to do anything asked of them, when the vision is strong and clear, but when the vision fades, as it too soon does, that is an end for them. Yet life without any vision, any looking forward and belief in better things to come, is dull and drab.

Linking Up the Task and the Vision of Life.—

A close study of this story of Martha and Mary seems to lead to the conclusion that this was the lesson, under the surface, that Jesus wanted to teach.

A woman with a task and no vision is a drudge.

A woman with a vision and no task is a visionary.

The vision and the task must be combined to get the best results.

"The highest character is the fruit of an ideal which is also a living force."

The practical woman is needed and also the woman with a vision. But better yet, let the practical woman take on a vision and the visionary woman take on the practical.

Some popular proverbs are wrong. It is said— "That you must not count your chickens before they are hatched;" but the farmer's wife who does not count — look after the eggs and the setting hens — her chickens before they are hatched will have no chickens. Again, it is said that —"You must not build castles in the air," but the woman who does not look ahead and plan what she wants to be and do, will never amount to anything.

The architect sees in vision the great building he is going to draw, and to erect, before he touches pencil to paper to make his plans. Edison saw, as in vision, the electric light and then he hunted around until he made it practical. It is related of Michael Angelo, that he wanted a block of marble at one time, to make a statue. He went to the quarries to find it. Half way there he saw a big block of marble which had been rejected because of angularity and certain defects. He had it sent to his studio, against the protests of the master of the quarries, who said that it was no good. But Angelo saw in it, as in a vision, the splendid statue of the David, one of the art wonders of the world. Here he had vision and task combined.

A Conclusion. When Jesus was on earth He was very practical in His teachings of the " Sermon on the Mount " and in His doing of good works, in the healing of the sick, but He also gave a great picture, in vision, of the future of what He expected His kingdom to accomplish. He looked to the far distant as well as the near future and spoke of the " Kingdom of Heaven " as spreading over the whole earth. It may have been that Mary in Martha's house, when she heard Him tell of these large plans and visions of the future, was fascinated and carried away by them and, the time passing quickly, forgot about the household duties. Martha, who was busy about the house, did not hear, and, missing the vision, chided her sister. In Martha and Mary, at the death and resurrection of their brother, Lazarus, we see that each one has learned what each one needed, to rightly interpret the task and the vision.

Questions.—What can be said of Martha's house? Give an account of a hostess' treatment of her guest; the conditions of oppression of Martha; a direct complaint; a request for interference in a family affair; the rebuke of Jesus; the attitude of Mary. Give a reason for Martha's action. What can be said of seeing life as a task; the Martha way? What can be said of seeing life as a vision; the Mary way? What can be said of linking up the task and the vision of life? The conclusion; as Jesus would have us see things.

XVII

MARY MAGDALENE

A WOMAN OF LARGE SERVICE

At the Front for Service.—Mary Magdalene, with her band of women of which she was the head, occupies a very prominent place in the Gospel narrative. They were foremost in ministering to Jesus Christ of their substance and personal help, in His aggressive campaigns in Galilee. They were with His company on the last journey to Jerusalem. They stood by at the cross. They were at the tomb. Mary was the first to see Christ after He rose from the dead. They took the initiative in doing good works. They never spared themselves in their efforts to forward the cause in which they so thoroughly believed. This was something new for women.

Mary was the Pioneer of the innumerable companies of modern women who are doing such a large service in supporting and pushing every good cause in our own day. In her time women were in seclusion. The place of the Oriental woman was in the rear. Through Mary's example and leadership we now see woman " At the front for service " in the church, philanthropic, educational, social and other matters. Where the light of the Gospel does not shine we still see the women relegated to the rear. We too often forget these facts and their significance.

Career of Mary Magdalene.—She is mentioned, by name, fourteen times in the Gospels—Luke 8: 2, 3 ; Matthew 27: 55, 56; Mark 15: 40, 41 ; John 19: 25 ; Matthew 27: 61 ; Matthew 28: 1 ; Mark 15: 47 ; Mark

16:1; Mark 16:9; compare Luke 24:10; John 20:1; John 20:11; John 20:16; John 20:18.

Leadership. A careful study of the above Scripture passages reveals very clearly what Mary did and how she did it.

In eight of the fourteen passages, where her name is mentioned, in connection with the other women, it always heads the list. This carefulness in always putting her name first must have been with the idea of showing her place at the front for service.

In five of the fourteen, her name is mentioned alone. These are all concerned with the important fact of the first appearance of Christ to her, after He had risen from the dead—Mark 16:9; John 20:1, 11, 16, 18.

In one of the fourteen, her name is mentioned after that of the mother and aunt of Jesus—John 19:25. This is where she stood close by the cross with these women, when Christ was crucified, and it would hardly have been right to have put her name before theirs.

The Name, Magdalene, is derived from Migdol, a watch tower. The place is now known as Mejdel, at the south of the plain of Gennesaret, where the hills approach the lake. This was near the center of our Lord's active ministry in Galilee.

Character. It is hardly possible for Mary to have had her high standing and to have formerly led the life of what is known as a " Magdalen."

The best New Testament scholars have entered a vigorous protest against the view of evil in Mary. They declare that she is not to be identified with the woman who was a sinner, in Luke 7:37-50, even if her name does come into the narrative, in the next chapter, in Luke 8:1-3. They declare that demoniacal possession, or a nervous disorder, of which she was cured by Christ, has nothing to do with badness of character. Here is a trouble that disturbs the mind and not the morals of a person. That Mary was sincerely grateful for her cure is shown by what she tried to do for Christ and His cause.

There are Five Situations in Which Mary's Largeness of Service Stands Out.—Women, especially Orientals, are the quickest to detect moral lapses on the part of their fellows. They would not have suffered her to lead them as she did, if there had been the slightest failure here.

She displays, in every situation, the very highest qualities of faith, fortitude, courage under trying circumstances, and unselfish love.

1—In Giving of Her Substance.—Sometimes women engaged in a cause, which they advocate most heartily, claim that, in giving their services free, they are, or ought to be, absolved from any pecuniary obligations. Not so Mary and her band.

Read what she did. The campaign of Jesus was at its height. "And it came to pass afterward that he (Jesus) went through every city and village, preaching and showing the glad tidings of the kingdom of God and the twelve were with him, and certain women which had been healed of evil spirits and infirmities, Mary, called Magdalene, out of whom went seven devils, and Joanna, the wife of Chuza, Herod's steward, and Susanna and many others which ministered unto him of their substance "—Luke 8:1-3.

Compare other passages where Mary's name is

mentioned as the first of the band and where like statements are made of these women ministering to Jesus—Matthew 27:55, 56; Mark 15:40, 41.

We never read of Jesus or His disciples taking up a collection or asking for money. Jesus is not recorded as ever having performed a miracle for the benefit of Himself. But money was necessary, then as now, for the support of those engaged in proclaiming the glad tidings.

Here we get a glimpse of generous women supplying campaign funds, without stint, for the carrying on of the work. It is expressly stated that they " Ministered unto him of their substance." Doubtless men contributed also but it was something new for women to give of their substance. There seems to have been no begging for money. Causes go very much better when people realize the need of funds and give without asking. These women had been benefited? Yes, certainly, but not all benefited ones are grateful. Christ once healed ten lepers and only one of them thanked Him. Mary was both grateful and generous.

2—In Personal Ministrations.—In moving about from place to place, as Jesus and His disciples did, there were many things that had to be looked after for their personal comfort and well-being. Some people had to look after the details and see that every thing went right. The life was much in the open air with a multitude of men, women and children about, who were strange to each other.

In order that there might be the right atmosphere, in which Christ could work, everything had to be kept in order and harmonious. In all this we see the work-

ing of Mary and her devoted band of women, ministering not only of their substance but contributing
much by their personal presence, in the best sort of
management, for the best results.

Would that this inside history, of which we get
glimpses, might have been written out more in detail!
There is also this same sort of inside history in every
modern church, where things go well, because there
are devoted women like Mary who go about quietly
and effectively in doing things, that need to be done,
and then say little or nothing about it.

3—In Difficult Special Service.—Causes do not
always go along smoothly no matter how well
managed. The highest hopes are often disappointed.
Jesus and His disciples in the latter part of His ministry, come to the hard part of the way.

Many of those whe seemed most heartily in His
favour, turn their backs upon Him. Crowds no
longer gather and hang upon His words. He has refused to pander to their worldly ambitions. Following Palm Sunday, when there has been a great
demonstration in His favour in Jerusalem, He is arrested and tried for His life. It is a time of testing.
Some of His most intimate friends and disciples leave
Him. He is condemned to death on the cross.

But Mary and her band do not desert Him. There
is no defection in their ranks. They follow and stand
probably as near the cross as they are allowed, although it seems "Afar off"—Matthew 27: 55, 56.
Physical suffering is not easy to look upon, yet these
women braved that, if perchance Jesus should lift
up His eyes, that He might see them.

If we turn now to John 19: 25 we notice that Mary

Magdalene is standing right by the cross, on which Jesus hangs in his death agony. She is with the mother and aunt of Jesus. What probably happened is this: Mary left the company of women, with which she was standing " Afar off," and gradually, as the darkness came on, worked her way down to a perilous position by the cross. She will, it seems, have Jesus see that the leader of His band of women, upon which He has relied, has not deserted Him but will stand by to the last. What more devoted service could there be than this?

Peter, the leader of the disciples, denied Christ at His trial, but Mary, the leader of the band of women, is right by the cross and cares not who sees her or identifies her with a lost cause, as it seems to be.

4—In Keeping Up Hope and Courage.—Even after Christ dies on the cross, and His body is taken down to be put in the tomb, " Mary Magdalene and the other Mary " take up a position near the tomb, Matthew 27:61, where they can see Jesus placed in His last earthly resting place. The disciples might have been there but there is no mention of it.

It is Mary Magdalene and her band who will see that everything is done that ought to be done for the body of Jesus, after it is placed in the tomb—Luke 23:55 to 24:1 and Matthew 28:1.

It is now that these women meet with an experience at first hand, which the world has not yet been able fully to grasp. The resurrection of Jesus! Who can understand this marvelous fact? We cannot wonder that these accounts, when everyone was trying to tell what was seen, are difficult to straighten out. In every great and startling event the same thing occurs and each one has a different story to tell, because each one sees a part and not the whole.

It is quite evident that the women, headed by Mary Magdalene—Luke 24 : 1-10, found the tomb empty. We are told that they were much perplexed and were afraid. Just then two men, in shining garments, stood by them, telling them that Jesus had risen from the dead; which doubtless perplexed them still more. But they did not express the doubt that the disciples did, Luke 24 : 10, 11. The accounts of Jesus' appearances to His disciples, belong in another chapter.

5—In Announcing the Greatest Good News That Has Ever Been Broadcast.—What could have been more fitting than that to Mary, and her faithful band of women, should have been given the task of first telling of the greatest event that the world has ever known!—Matthew 28 and Luke 24. They stood by when others had given up. They rendered a large service that meant not simply believing and working, when all was fair, but when there seemed not a ray of hope.

To Mary, as the foremost of the faithful band, was given the signal honour of being the first one to see her risen Lord—John 20 : 1-18.

Questions.—What can be said of Mary Magdalene? How was she a pioneer and in what? What can be said of her career; how many times is she mentioned; leadership; name; character? Describe the five situations in which Mary's largeness of service stands out? 1—In giving of her substance? 2—In personal ministrations? 3—In difficult special service? 4—In keeping up hope and courage? 5—In announcing the greatest good news that has ever been broadcast?

XVIII

MOTHER OF JAMES AND JOHN

AN AMBITIOUS WOMAN

The Incident, of which this study is the exposition, is found in Matthew 20: 20-28.

Jesus is on His last journey to Jerusalem. His disciples, the women who ministered to Him, and a great company, are with Him.

The mother of James and John, apostles, comes to Him with the singular request that they sit, one upon His right hand, and the other on the left, when He is enthroned. The other apostles are indignant at this appeal, for what seems to them, special favour. Jesus' reply, in regard to the nature of true ambition, is of more than passing interest. If it is ever universally accepted, and adopted, it will produce a radical change for betterment.

Salome, the wife of Zebedee, and the mother of his children, seems to have been a follower of Jesus from the beginning of His career.

She was an able and energetic woman of fine character. She was not a woman who kept her religion to herself but taught her sons in the way. Her example and teaching were such that they were glad to go along with their mother. There is a depth of devotion, a wide range of vision, and a joyousness in the writings of her sons which show that they were not forced into their religion but led by a mother who understood her boys. She was a faithful follower of Jesus Christ up to the very end—Matthew 27: 56; Mark 15: 40, 41; Mark 16: 1.

The Family Life was a Happy One.—Here were people who were not poor and not rich. Zebedee, the father, owned fishing boats and nets. He had hired servants—Matthew 4:21; Mark 1:19, 20. His sons worked with him until they were called to follow Jesus. It is not difficult to read between the lines of the harmony in this family in regard to what they did.

Capernaum, where the family lived, was no mean city. It was enough to stir any one's ambition to live here. It was at a world's crossroads. Caravans passed and repassed from the most distant centers of population. It was at the junction of four great central ways from Arabia, Egypt, Tyre and Damascus. What ever happened, in the world at large, was soon known in this city. It possessed a Roman garrison and was the headquarters for Roman government and taxation in all Galilee.

It was the principal place on the lake of Galilee, the shores of which were covered thickly with small cities and Roman villas. Jesus Christ made it His headquarters after His rejection at Nazareth. He could reach more people, and reach them more effectively, from this city than from any other place. Here He could talk about the world-wide nature of His kingdom with a large freedom, and this talk, with the surroundings, is evidently what stirred Salome to make her startling request.

An Ambitious Woman.—In what way? For what?

There are many types of women in the Bible. Because a woman's name is here is no sign that she is to be commended or condemned.

Intrd

Their stories are given and the mirror held up. It is for us to say how we like their looks. We have bad women like Jezebel and Delilah and there can be no worse. Good women like Ruth and Hannah. Able women like Deborah and Esther. Cruel women like Herodias and her daughter. Here they are, rich, poor, wise, ignorant, proud, humble, foolish, kindly and the reverse.

There is a whole host of them. They antedate by hundreds of years, modern characters yet, in other lands and under different circumstances, talk and act just like them. This is the value of this Bible study of women, because we can always find a type in the Scriptures of any modern woman, and see how she acted and we may be quite sure, under the guise of our present-day civilization, she will run true to the old form. Human nature seems to be the same in all lands and in all ages.

How does Salome look to us?

1. *Ambition.* There are almost as many kinds of ambition as there are types of women in the Bible. It plays no small part in the affairs of women as well as men. It seeks high and low objects and with almost equal enthusiasm. It leads to the heights of honour, and to the depths of degradation. It is right and it is wrong. It is noble and it is ignoble.

It all depends upon the motive and the object sought. Ambition, the desire and determination, to go ahead and to accomplish things, is a means to an end.

In itself it is a necessity if anyone is to get anywhere. The chief question is of its right employment.

The Great Request of Salome that her sons

now a request was not knew
for Jesus. 1. serve quietly
2. near 27.11
3 any for 11

should occupy the chief places, in the coming kingdom of Christ, was a very ambitious one. In this request she was seconded by James and John. They seemed to feel, if we read the narrative rightly, not the slightest reluctance or embarrassment in doing as they did.

How did she come to ask for this honour?

First. Consider Salome herself. She was a woman with a fine mind. She had a deeply devotional nature. She was endowed with large vision. She lived in no mean city where news came from the ends of the earth. She was accustomed to think in the large terms of the Roman empire. All the facts of her life point this way. She could realize on the future in a way in which few can. We are too prone to try to cramp the Bible characters back into small conceptions of things when we are told differently by the writers of the Gospel narratives. Here was fertile soil for a large ambition.

Second. Christ himself. He constantly talked about the largeness of His kingdom; " The Kingdom of God " and " The Kingdom of Heaven." He never spoke of " The Kingdom of the Jews." His Gospel was to be world-wide. He did not speak of preaching to any one particular nation, but " All nations." His was to be a universal and an everlasting kingdom. The Gospels are full of references to Christ's Kingdom—Matthew 3:2; 8:11; 11:11; 13:11; Matthew 5:3; 7:21; Luke 9:62; John 3:3; Parables of the Kingdom, Matthew 13. See also Matthew 24 and 25. He said to His disciples at the last, " Go ye therefore and teach all nations," Matthew 28:19. See also Luke 24:47, 48 and Acts 1:8. The largest possible conception of His mission is given repeatedly to His followers, not privately but publicly. This was the seed that fell into the fertile soil of Salome's mind.

The Circumstances of the Request. Christ and His company were going up to Jerusalem. It was His last journey, just before His trial and crucifixion which He plainly foretold—Matthew 20: 17-19.

Notwithstanding what Christ said of His crucifixion, it might have seemed to Salome, the mother of Zebedee's children, that, in some way and somehow, His kingdom, of which she had heard so much, would be realized in the sacred city of Jerusalem. It might have been also that she had been so fired with the idea of the greatness of Christ's kingdom and had seen Him do so many wonderful things that it seemed to her that there could be no failure. She could not see the necessity for this step of crucifixion and death and resurrection in order that the largeness of the kingdom might be realized.

Hence her great ambition that her sons might rule with Christ, one sitting on the right and the other on the left hand. It shows her faith, and its strength, that she asked for what she did at the time she did.

The Indignation of the Apostles.—Some New Testament scholars think that some of this indignation came from the fact that they had not thought to make this request first. They certainly expressed themselves vigorously against Salome and her sons. It may have seemed to them that she had taken an undue advantage.

The Answer of Christ to the request. He asks James and John if they are able to endure with Him the hardships of the kingdom in drinking of His cup of woe and being baptized with His baptism. They reply that they are. He then replies that they will drink of His cup and be baptized with His baptism, but that the seats on His right and left are not His to bestow upon them, but that the Father will give them to those for whom they are prepared.

He now seems to gather to Him His apostles and Salome, and to talk to them on the true nature of His kingdom and the proper kind of ambition that should be exercised toward it.

First. Christ speaks of the selfish ambition that gets into the hearts of men and drives them on to get all they can, in all the ways they can, for themselves, and themselves only, without a thought or care for others. In this He uses the illustration of the princes of the Gentiles who exercise authority for gain. Here is raised the whole question of the desire to exploit others to get on in the world. He points out the danger involved.

Second. He speaks of the motive of a true ambition and what should govern it. This underlies the " Sermon on the Mount " and His whole Gospel. It is all summed up in one word, " Serve." It is ministering for others. It is looking out for others as you look out for yourself and your own interests—" Whosoever will be great among you, let him be your minister; And whosoever will be chief among you, let him be your servant; Even as the Son of man came not to be ministered unto but to minister and to give his life a ransom for many "—Matthew 20: 25-28.

The Rule of the Christ, the third (see below), which He presented to Salome and her sons, is the only one which can bring happiness.

There are three classes of people in the world and

if you look you can find them with very little difficulty. They are each using a certain rule of life.

First Rule. Get all you can and give back as little as you can. This is the brass rule of life. It works for hardship and misery always. For the person who uses it, is almost sure to be repaid in kind, but he does not like his own rule applied to himself.

Second Rule. Give an exact equivalent. For a kind word, give a kind word. For a hard word, give one back. Get even with everyone. Do not let any one get the better of you. Watch out and see that you get your dues, no matter who suffers. Push for the first place, no matter who is hurt, so long as you get it; for is not everyone doing it? This is getting even.

Third Rule. Do a little more than is expected of you. Be a little kinder than the man next to you, than he is to you. Go out of your way to do a favour where no one thinks of your doing it. No one thought of Jesus Christ coming to this earth to save men or help them in any way. See John 3:16. This third rule is the very heart of Christ's advice on ambition— " Whosoever will be chief among you, let him be your servant "—Matthew 20: 26, 27.

Questions.—What can be said of the incident of which this study is an exposition? What can be said of Salome? What was the family life? Describe Capernaum. What can be said of an ambitious woman? What was the great request of Salome; the first and second points and the circumstances? The indignation of the apostles? The answer of Christ; the first and second points? The rule of Christ, contrast the first and second with the third.

XIX

DORCAS

A PHILANTHROPIC WOMAN

The Fame of Dorcas, as a worker in the philanthropic field, has filled the whole world with its fragrance.

This woman's movement, for the good of others, in unselfish service, begun in the little city of Joppa, has flowed out beyond the bounds of the early church into a multitude of benevolent and charitable organizations. In these, women have been the most prominent.

Let us give credit, where credit is due, to this woman disciple whose religious belief impelled her to organize this sort of work which was unknown and uncared for before her time.

The Story, of " Good works and almsdeeds," is very brief. It is comprised in seven short verses in the Book of Acts—9: 36-42.

" Now there was at Joppa a certain disciple named Tabitha, which by interpretation is called Dorcas; this woman was full of good works and almsdeeds which she did. And it came to pass in those days, that she was sick and died; whom when they had washed, they laid her in an upper chamber. And for as much as Lydda was nigh to Joppa, and the disciples had heard that Peter was there, they sent unto him two men, desiring him that he would not

142   Studies of Famous Bible Women

delay to come to them.   Then Peter arose and went
with them.   When he was come, they brought him
into the upper chamber: and all the widows stood by
him weeping, and showing the coats and garments
which Dorcas made, while she was with them.   But
Peter put them all forth, and kneeled down, and
prayed; and turning him to the body said, Tabitha
arise.   And she opened her eyes: and when she saw
Peter, she sat up.   And he gave her his hand, and
lifted her up, and when he had called the saints and
widows, presented her alive.   And it was known
throughout all Joppa and many believed in the Lord."

The Ancient City of Joppa was about thirty
five miles from Jerusalem.   It was never very large.
It was built on a rocky eminence about 116 feet above
the level of the sea.   The remains of the house of
Tabitha are pointed out to the traveler who visits this
place.

Standing in Life.—Judging from the narrative,
that of Dorcas must have been good.   She was evidently a woman who owned her own home and had
sufficient money to do as she liked.   She does not
seem to have had any near relatives.   In fact no
relative is mentioned.   When she died quite suddenly,
and had been properly laid out, the widows, whom she
had helped, crowded the upper room where she was.
Peter, the apostle, having been sent for, soon made
his appearance and was shown the coats and garments which had been made by this good woman and
given away.   This was a fine eulogy of her practical
work.   When Peter had restored Tabitha to life, she
doubtless continued in the same way of good deeds.

What She Did and How.—She was an intensive worker. She took up a particular cause, in a special way, and put her whole heart, and all her energy into it. Nothing is said of her faith, save that she was " A certain disciple." There is no account of her conversion. Our attention is held, strictly, to her eminence in " Almsdeeds and good works " and here she is pre-eminent. Faith is shown in action.

Work in Her Own Home.—When we read the Gospels and Acts, we cannot help but note the fact of the constant moving about from place to place, and city to city, of the early Christian workers. They never seem to be still. They come and they go. They accomplish great things in this way. The impression might be easily gained that this is the only way of doing what ought to be done in the carrying out of the commands of the Christ.

Here is shown another way. Dorcas remained in her own home, where the possibilities were very limited. There seemed to be no wide outlook.

If she ever longed for a larger sphere of action it is not evident in her story. Here was her standing place from which she would move the world. She was not without ambition to do large things but it was an ambition to stand just where she was and do them most effectively.

A new note is sounded, in the Gospel proclamation, of intensive home work.

Cheerfulness.—There are those who do their whole duty in a limited sphere but to them it is a hard and rigorous one. There is no joy in it. Those who come in contact with such women feel this rigour.

Dorcas was a woman of good cheer. How do we

know? Because of the action of the widows. A good deed may be like throwing a bone to a dog which hits him. The dog resents it while feeling compelled to take the bone. Benevolence of this sort gets no thanks. When Dorcas died the widows crowded around weeping and showing the garments which she had made. Here was the response that comes from cheerfulness, in giving, and can come in no other way.

A real philanthropist gets as close as she can to the subject of her good deed. This is, in fact, the only true philanthropy. It is the only kind that elicits any real gratitude.

Plying Her Own Needle.—The widows showed the coats and garments which Dorcas had made with her own hands. This was personal work. It required thought and care. She put into what she did something of herself. There are those who give to benevolences out of more or less abundant means. They can easily spare what they give. The check is sent and there is rather a warm glow about the heart that something has been done to relieve some one poorer off than themselves. But there is no personal touch in it. It is not known exactly where the money goes or how it is spent.

Dorcas seems to have had a personal acquaintance with those for whom she made garments. These garments were not gathered up, as "Castoffs," but were made and fitted by the donor. That they were well made, and looked well on those who wore them, is evident from the pride with which the widows showed them to Peter. No woman cares to exhibit an ill fitting garment to anyone. Doubtless the widows had come to Dorcas' home and had "Try-ons."

Here is a fundamental principle, in philanthropy, that the gift should be fitted to the one who is to receive it. The neglect of this principle is the cause of much dissatisfaction. The donor wonders why her gift is received with so little gratitude and the recipient is out of sorts because she cannot make use of that which has been given.

Leadership.—One of the most stressed things in our day is "Leadership." Our young women are exhorted to strive to be leaders and to fit themselves for it. It is an appeal which makes a strong impression on pride. The many forms of social and philanthropic service are the chosen fields pointed out for leadership. In this leadership the chosen one is to plan and lay out the work, while others are to follow and carry out her directions. This idea is very attractive and wins many.

The great trouble is to get followers for all the leaders who are trained for it. We are raising up an army of generals in which there are no privates. The disappointment of the generals, who get no army to lead, is naturally great.

Dorcas did not aspire to be a leader. She just did the philanthropic work in her own house which was right at her hand. Her ambition seems to have been to do all that she could in all the ways that she could. In this way, in spite of herself, she has become a great woman leader in philanthropic work. She was the great pioneer. In this short narrative of her life and work are to be found the great principles on which this work is to be done, if it is successful.

All real leadership is and must be founded on personal service. It cannot be taught entirely in the schools. It must be established on great qualities of heart and mind. These qualities, exercised for the good of humanity, lift one to true leadership. This is the cause of the exaltation of Dorcas. She did not lift herself up but was lifted up by the intensity of her devotion to an ideal which found the highest service starting right in her own home. The life history of every great leader, points out this as the way.

Friendship.—Little good can be done in philanthropic work without the establishment of friendly relations between the giver and the recipient of the gift. Where articles, or money, are given without these friendly relations, they may relieve physical wants; they do; but they pauperize the spirit and make, in the end, the condition of the recipient worse than it was before. Those who come to ask for things are not helped in any real way and benevolence becomes a positive harm. This is now everywhere acknowledged.

Dorcas established friendly relations between herself and those whom she helped out of their difficulties. The widows would never have come and wept over her, after she was dead, if this had not been the case. They, if there had been no friendly relations, would have remained away. With Dorcas dead, there was nothing more to be hoped for. Again they thought so much of Dorcas, who had done so much for them, that they sent for Peter to see if he could not help them, and he did.

The aid in true friendship is as much, if not more, than any material assistance that can be given.

A Great Opportunity came to Dorcas, right in her own home, in a small city of Palestine. She is known throughout the world as the organizer of the Dorcas Society for the exercise of the New Philanthropy; but Dorcas did not start out to found any new society. She seemed, in fact, unconscious of the splendid work which she was doing. She wanted to do something for her Lord and just did that which first came to her hand, and did it in the most simple way. This is the sort of thing, after all, that is going to raise humanity to a higher level. It is just doing the thing next at hand and doing it to the best of our ability, that is the great opportunity for all of us.

Questions.—What can be said of the fame of Dorcas? Where is her story found? Give the story. Give her standing in life. What did she do and how did she do it? What can be said of her work in her own home? What of her cheerfulness? What can be said of her plying her needle? What of her leadership? What of friendship? What can be said of her great opportunity?

XX

MARY, MOTHER OF MARK

AN INFLUENTIAL CHURCH WORKER

There are a number of Marys mentioned in the Gospels, Mary, the mother of Jesus, Mary Magdalene and others, but Mary, the mother of Mark, is spoken of but once, Acts 12:12; "And when he (Peter) had considered the thing, he came to the house of Mary, the mother of John, whose surname was Mark; where many were gathered together praying." This brief description tells us a good deal about her life, character and work. Read Acts 12:1-19.

There was a Crisis in the career of Christianity. It is told in the twelfth chapter of Acts. At the first, everything seemed to go well. Large numbers of people gave their allegiance to The Christ. The Jews became alarmed. "The Crucified One" seemed to be making greater progress than when He was on earth. A persecution arose which had for its object, the stamping out of this religion. James, the brother of John, was killed with the sword. Then Peter, who was the head and front of the Christ movement, was taken and put in prison.

The Turning Point, for Better Things, was in the house of Mary, the mother of Mark. This energetic and forceful woman was not content to let things drift. She, when she saw how affairs were moving, seems to have summoned the leading Christians in the

148

city to her home, and laid the situation before them. It was a time to try their souls. So far as bringing any pressure to bear for the release of Peter, they were helpless. James had been killed and Peter seemed destined to bear the same fate. If matters went on, as they were going, few, if any, Christians would be left.

Long and earnest debate might have taken place in regard to what to do and how to do it. Mary, the leading spirit in this conference, as she is the only person mentioned, doubtless suggested the appeal to a " Higher Power " above that of the persecutors and Herod, the king.

This appeal was made. Most earnest prayer was offered up for Peter's release. Even while they prayed Peter was let out of prison and came knocking at the door of the gate. Such a sudden and startling answer to their prayers was, at first, unbelievable. But Peter continued knocking until they were convinced of his presence.

The success of this prayer meeting, in the home of this influential church worker, cannot be overestimated. We turn to the next chapter, the thirteenth, and read of the beginning of the mighty missionary movement that has encircled the earth.

The House of Mary was of some considerable size. This is argued from the fact that " Many were gathered together praying." It was quite a large household with a number of maids of whom Rhoda, who went to answer Peter's knocking at the door, was but one. It is supposed that Mary was a widow with means. The location, doubtless a prominent one, was well known. There is an old tradition that this house was the scene of " The Last Supper." The hospitality of Mary was well known to Peter. When he was released from prison, he made his way at once to this home where he was sure of receiving a welcome and of finding his friends.

Forceful Character.—Mary was brought up, bound in all the traditions of Oriental women. By these she must be veiled when she goes abroad. She must live in a certain seclusion. As a widow, she must only receive women into her home. She must not take part in public affairs. On no account must she make her home a public meeting place. When she became a Christian she broke utterly with these traditions.

She makes her home a rallying place for what was to many a despised sect. She is a propagandist for that in which she believes. She holds this new faith not as a means of breaking down an old one, but as a step by which to go on up to higher and better things. She sees in the new freedom, which has come to her, not an avenue to license to do that which is unlawful, but as a new way for a larger happiness to everyone. The natural strength of her character now has an opportunity to reveal itself under her profession of Christ.

The High Position which Mary attained would have been possible under no other religion and under no other circumstances. This Christian religion, at once, began her emancipation and made her a leader in the affairs of life. We see women coming to the front to-day for the same reason. They are winning the high places as church, professional, industrial, commercial, social and civic workers because of what

Christ said and did for them. To be sure some of them may say that they have attained these through other means but the fact remains true that it is only under the Christian religion that women have these large opportunities.

Courage.—We must not forget that it took great bravery to do what Mary did. She had to take her stand with a comparatively few against what public opinion allowed and did not allow for women. She might have secretly professed Christianity and let it go at that. But to come out and to take an active part, as she did, was quite another matter. She must have alienated many old time friends. The big house and the wealth which Mary had were obstacles in the way of her taking an active part. She probably invited confiscation of property and forfeit of her life by her Christian activity, but she was not to be deterred.

The instance given, in Acts 12:12, shows this courage, of this rare sort, in a very interesting way. Mary opened her home to a public meeting for her fellow Christians when a great persecution was at its height and Christianity seemed about to perish from the earth. Some think that the hesitation of Rhoda, who went to the door when Peter, coming from prison, knocked for admission, was due to the fact that she thought it was the soldiers of Herod, who had come to arrest those in the house.

Inspirer of Men Who Did Valiant Service.— We know some of the things that came out of the house of Mary. We are quite certain of them. Some of them we have set down. Note this list of men:

Peter. How much did Mary influence him and encourage him? We know this that he must have been encouraged by her, for he, when he was released from prison, at once made his way to her home.

Mark. Her own son. He went on the first missionary journey with Barnabas and Saul, afterwards called Paul. He was with Peter on his travels. He was also, at another time, with Paul. He wrote, as the interpreter of Peter, what is known as the Gospel of Mark. He certainly had an opportunity to know about things, at first hand, in his mother's home.

Barnabas. Mary's nephew. He was very active in the days of the beginnings of the Christian Church. He went to Tarsus and got Saul to go to Antioch, where he did such a wonderful work. He went on the first missionary journey with Saul. He, afterwards, went on a mission himself.

We only get a glimpse of this work with and for men by Mary, but it is enough to show its exceedingly great importance.

Originator of the Home Prayer Meeting—Was she? It certainly looks like it. Christ spoke in the Jewish synagogues and out in the open. The apostles and early Christian teachers sought at first to speak in the synagogues, but the radical differences developed soon caused them to seek the homes of their disciples and to build churches. But Mary wanted the Christian service in her own home. She evidently had confidence in what could be done with a "Home Prayer Meeting." Her confidence was justified. This meeting as a means of getting and transmitting spiritual power cannot be overestimated.

The writers of the epistles frequently speak of these meetings or " House Churches."

Interpreter of the Ideals of Love, Loyalty and Service.—If Mary had been possessed of scant love she would not have undertaken the hazardous service of opening her home to a persecuted sect. She was loyal to her Christian ideals. She did not falter in her service, although she knew that it might lead to the destruction of all she had and forfeiting her life.

The truest, strongest women of which any community may boast are, for the most part, those who give to the church self-sacrificing thought and time and effort in the service of their Lord and their fellow men and women. This work is done in many ways in the church, Sunday school, and social service.

Questions.—Are there other Marys mentioned in the Gospels? How many times is Mary, the mother of Mark, spoken of? What can be said of the crisis of Christianity, at this time? When and where was the turning point for better things? What can be said of the house of Mary? Describe the forceful character of Mary. What can be said of her high position; her courage? How is she the inspirer of men? Was she the originator of the home prayer meeting? What can be said of Mary as an interpreter of the ideals of love, loyalty and service?

XXI

LYDIA

A BUSINESS WOMAN

Lydia was a successful business woman in a prosperous city. She was the forerunner of the modern business and professional woman. They, the old and new types, have the same characteristics; alert, capable, knowing what they want to do and doing it with large ability, enthusiasm, and singleness of purpose.

Read the story in Acts 16:12-40 and specially verses 12, 13, 14, 15 and 40.

Birthplace.—Thyatira, a city of one of the provinces of Asia. This was her dwelling place for a number of years.

Occupation.—"A seller of purple." She doubtless removed from her native city in order that she might enlarge her business.

The Opportunity in Thyatira was Small, for a dealer, as it was a manufacturing city. It was famous for its extensive dye works. " Purple was a favourite colour with the ancients. This included shades ranging all the way from rose red to sea green and blue. The dye which yielded the colouring matter was procured from the gland of a certain shell fish. Lydia may have been merchandising the dye or the cloth, which had passed through the colouring process, or both."

154

The Opportunity in Philippi was Large, for a dealer, as it was a big commercial city. It was the metropolis of Macedonia. It was a good copy of Rome in its architecture, life and manners. As a meeting place of the East and West it was daily visited by throngs of strangers who came and went by the great Egnatian Highway. Lydia showed her excellent business sense in coming to this city where she could reach so many more people.

Here she prospered greatly. She was able to do a large business in spite of keen competition.

A Woman in Business was a thing unheard of for an Oriental. But Lydia in turning to Judaism had adopted an entirely different set of ideals as to what a woman could and could not do. Every avenue of life was now open to her. She had before her the picture of the possibilities of a business life for a woman as it had been depicted, long before her time, in the Book of Proverbs, 31 : 10-31. Here a woman is described, not only as a good housekeeper, but as buying and selling on her own account without consulting anyone. She manufactures goods. She deals in real estate. She gives her opinion on affairs and it is heeded. While she is a good wife and mother, she is also an important factor in all that goes on outside.

Religion.—Lydia not only had a keen business mind by which she was able to meet and overcome the sharp competition of the Philippian traders, but also a deeply spiritual nature which she allowed to control her. She took her religion seriously. It was something to be looked after as closely as her business interests.

First, We Meet with Her as a Jewish Proselyte.
We do not know when she became a convert but she
was very much in earnest about it. That there were
so few Jews in Philippi that they were unable to have
a synagogue made no difference to Lydia. She found
a few women of this faith and with them she went to
the river bank, out of the city, and held a service of
worship and prayer.

It took moral courage to shut up her shop, when
everyone else kept open, and go with so few to keep
the Sabbath day. She might very easily have said
that she could worship in her own heart and be in
readiness for any trade that came her way, with an
open shop. But that was not her way. If her
religion was worth anything, it was worth everything to her.

Second, We See Her as a Christian Convert. Paul,
on his second missionary journey, came to Philippi,
searching for a large center of population where he
might preach the Gospel. It was the policy then to
attack the strongholds, the great cities, and having
planted the seed, to let it grow large and spread to the
surrounding country. Christianity was not at all
timid in making its claims known. It was bold and
aggressive because it was believed that it had the only
life giving power through its Christ. But Paul could
not find any Jewish synagogue in the city and the synagogue was the place where he usually began his campaign. He was forced to go out of the city to find
anything resembling a place of worship of God and
here he found Lydia with a few women. Her " Heart
the Lord opened that she attended unto the things
which were spoken of Paul."

She has the honour of being the first European convert; the forerunner of a great host who have done valiant service for their Master. She was wholehearted in her conversion. She, at once, wanted to do something to help and invited Paul and his company to be her guests.

Environment.—It was bad. There was no encouragement for religion or morality in Philippi. As Rome had lost her faith in her gods, so this city. Death was regarded as an eternal sleep. There was no hereafter to be dreaded or hoped for. The policy was to live while you live and to squeeze all the pleasure possible out of this world; it was forgotten that in doing this that it was the doer who suffered.

The amusements, for the people, in the city amphitheater were cruel to the last degree; men fought with wild beasts, and with their fellow men, to the death. The people, with their depraved tastes, demanded this sort of thing. Morality was a jest.

It was no easy thing for a prominent woman merchant to stand out against this, but Lydia did it. She seems to have prospered wonderfully in her business as she did in her religion. There is much in being true to one's principles; for they command the respect of those who have no principles of their own.

Lydia was not a product of her environment.

Faithfulness and Humility.—It is sometimes said that contact with the world of business hardens women and that they lose their charm as women. They are disillusionized in many ways and they show their disillusionment. Lydia had no easy proposition along this line. She dealt with men who gave no quarter.

Lydia witnesses for herself as to how she kept her charm of faithfulness and humility. The writer of The Acts says—"And when she was baptized, and her household, she besought us saying, If ye have judged me to be faithful to the Lord, come into my house and abide there. And she constrained us." She might have assumed an entirely different attitude of arrogance and told Paul that he ought to consider himself honoured to be invited to the home of one of the leading merchants of the city.

All honour to this woman living and doing business in this city, that she did not lose her womanliness.

Dependability.—There are many men and women expert in business. They profess to be just in their dealings. They are shrewd buyers and sellers. They understand thoroughly the goods in which they deal. They are fine judges of values, but those who deal with them are very wary in regard to what they say about their goods. They have all knowledge, but use that knowledge to get the better of their customers. They are not to be depended upon.

Lydia must have been an excellent judge of goods and of values. She had to be to do business and succeed in Philippi. The fine thing about the narrative of this woman is the atmosphere of dependability. You feel that if you had lived in those times in that city that you could have gone into the store of Lydia and said, "I want so much of purple dye, I have so much money to spend. You take this money and give me its value." You would have been sure that you would get all the dye that was coming to you and a little more. We begin to see why Lydia was so successful and why she held her customers, even if she did not do as others and keep open on her Sabbath.

She was thoroughly reliable and that sort of reputation pays large dividends in business and in religion. She stood by Paul and Silas under adverse conditions. Right after " The River Bank Meeting " they went to prayer again, probably the next day, and on the way they healed a half demented girl. For this good act they were cast into prison and their feet made fast in the stocks. On being released in the morning, Lydia is on hand with the offer of her home for them. She could be depended upon to stand by when misfortune came upon her friends.

Cheerfulness.—Life presents many hard aspects. Business is beset with thorny difficulties. We cannot escape these things. They are always present. Especially does a life of business, for a woman, tend to wipe from her face the cheerful smile. There are so many things to irk her, even in modern days, where so many women are employed in stores and offices. The low wages and the long hours for some make a rocky pathway wherein to walk. But the situation is never helped by the glooms; it is only made worse.

Here, in this narrative, we notice again another element, and that is of cheerfulness. There is no word of the hardships which beset Lydia. If she had them, as had them she must, they are not mentioned. There is no word of complaint of being compelled to worship on the river bank.

When Paul and Silas are put in prison for doing a good deed, after the conversion of Lydia, they sing songs. Strange, is it not, that these men beaten, with their feet bound fast in the stocks, should sing songs!

Self-Respect.—Lydia had come up from Thyatira, her home town, where every one knew her, and where she was under certain restraints, to Philippi to business on a larger scale. She might have said that this is a great city where things are done in a different way and I can just let my old scruples go. Then, too, I want to get new business and I must work for it in all the ways I can, even if I go to places where I ought not.

The call and the lure of Bohemia Land is just as loud and strong as it ever was. The mocking laughter that greets those who refuse to enter is just as loud, if not louder, than ever. Why not yield? Why persist in puritan principles and scruples? There were wits in those days who doubtless made a lot of sport of Lydia, who would go to a prayer meeting on a river bank instead of going with them to Bohemia Land. But there seemed to be no regrets on Lydia's part that she did not go. It was no hardship for her to stay away. Her safeguards were inside, not outside.

She knew, apart from business and religious reasons, that the one great thing lost in Bohemia Land is one's own respect. One is never the same after losing that immediate jewel of the soul. When one fails to respect one's self, there is not much left.

Questions.—What can be said about Lydia as a successful business woman? Birthplace? Occupation? A woman in business? What can be said of Lydia's religion? Lydia as a Jewish proselyte? As a Christian convert? What can be said of the environment of Lydia? Her faithfulness and humility? Her dependability? Her cheerfulness? Her self-respect?

THE END